Security for Microsoft Windows System Administrators

Security for Microsoft Windows System Administrators

Introduction to Key Information Security Concepts

Derrick Rountree

Rodney Buike, Technical Editor

ELSEVIER

AMSTERDAM • BOSTON • HEIDELBERG • LONDON
NEW YORK • OXFORD • PARIS • SAN DIEGO
SAN FRANCISCO • SINGAPORE • SYDNEY • TOKYO
Syngress is an imprint of Elsevier

SYNGRESS®

Acquiring Editor: Angelina Ward
Development Editor: Heather Scherer
Project Manager: Paul Gottehrer
Designer: Alisa Andreola

Syngress is an imprint of Elsevier
30 Corporate Drive, Suite 400, Burlington, MA 01803, USA

Notices
Knowledge and best practice in this field are constantly changing. As new research and experience broaden our understanding, changes in research methods or professional practices, may become necessary. Practitioners and researchers must always rely on their own experience and knowledge in evaluating and using any information or methods described herein. In using such information or methods they should be mindful of their own safety and the safety of others, including parties for whom they have a professional responsibility.

To the fullest extent of the law, neither the Publisher nor the authors, contributors, or editors, assume any liability for any injury and/or damage to persons or property as a matter of products liability, negligence or otherwise, or from any use or operation of any methods, products, instructions, or ideas contained in the material herein.

Library of Congress Cataloging-in-Publication Data
Application submitted

British Library Cataloguing-in-Publication Data
A catalogue record for this book is available from the British Library.

ISBN: 978-1-59749-594-3

Printed in the United States of America
10 11 12 13 14   10 9 8 7 6 5 4 3 2 1

Typeset by: diacriTech, Chennai, India

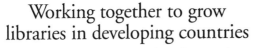

For information on all Syngress publications visit our website at *www.syngress.com*

Dedication

This book is dedicated to my daughter Riley, my grandmother Rosa, and my great grandmother Mary.

CONTENTS

Acknowledgments

First, I would like to thank my wife Michelle. We are heading down the new road of parenthood together. It's both exciting and a little bit scary. I would like to thank my mother Claudine, my sister Kanesha, and my grandmother Lugenia. Thank you for being there for me. I would also like to thank my two best friends Carrie and Fela. The two of you have shown me what true friendship is. You've also served as examples of persistence and dedication. Because of you, I know the road may be long, but if you stick with it, eventually you will get to your destination. I love you all.

Finally, I would like to thank the Elsevier staff, especially Angelina Ward, Senior Acquisitions Editor and Heather Scherer, Developmental Editor. It has truly been a pleasure working with you.

About the Author

Derrick Rountree (CISSP, Security +, MCSE, MCSA) has been in the IT field for over 16 years. He has a Bachelors of Science in Electrical Engineering. Derrick has held positions as a network administrator, IT consultant, and QA engineer. He has experience in network security, operating system security, application security, and secure software development. Derrick has contributed to several other Syngress and Elsevier publications on Citrix, Microsoft, and Cisco technologies.

Tech Editor

Rodney Buike (MCSE) is an IT pro advisor with Microsoft Canada. As an IT pro advisor, Rodney spends his day helping IT professionals in Canada with issues and challenges they face in their environment and careers. He also advocates for a stronger community presence and shares knowledge through blogging, podcasts, and in-person events.

Rodney's specialties include Exchange Server, virtualization, and core infrastructure technologies on the Windows platform. Rodney worked as a LAN administrator, system engineer, and consultant and has acted as a reviewer on many popular technical books. Rodney is also the founder and principal content provider for Thelazyadmin.com and a former author for MSExchange.org.

INTRODUCTION TO GENERAL SECURITY CONCEPTS

INFORMATION IN THIS CHAPTER

- Principles of Information Security
- Information Security Standards, Regulations, and Compliance
- Authentication, Authorization, and Accounting (AAA)
- Access Control

A company's most important asset next to its people is its information. This information includes intellectual property, company financial information, confidential employee information, customer information, and so much more. Company information may be stored in databases, spreadsheets, flat files, and so on. Loss of company information can be very costly and in some cases devastating to a company. In many cases, this devastation can not only come from the lost information but also be just the fact that information was lost. When a company loses information, the company may also lose its reputation. For example, if customer credit card information is lost, customers may lose confidence that the company is safe to do business with. We've all seen in the news where companies have suffered a breach and customer card information was stolen. How eager were you to do business with that company after hearing about the loss? Probably not very eager, right? It can take months, even years, for a company to gain back the confidence of its customers. In some cases, companies suffer permanent and irreparable damage. They never fully gain back the customer base they once had. As an administrator, you must do everything possible to protect your company's information. This protecting of company information is called *information security*.

As you will learn, information security is not an easy topic to deal with. This isn't because it's not possible to completely secure your environment, as some people would lead you to believe.

Security for Microsoft Windows System Administrators. DOI: 10.1016/B978-1-59749-594-3.00001-6

1

It's quite the opposite. The difficulty comes in the fact that it is possible to completely lock down your environment so that there can be no security breaches. All you have to do is store all your information on one or two systems. Next, ensure that these systems are not connected to any network. And finally, lock the systems in a room where only you have the key. Now your job is done, right? Of course, it isn't. Part of your job as an administrator is to make company information available to those who need it. This is where the difficulty comes in. In making company information and systems available for access by others, you are inherently making your environment less secure. What you are then faced with is the age-old compromise between security and usability. You have to make your environment secure, but at the same time, you have to make sure it is usable. Striking the right balance can be very difficult task. But having a good understanding of security measures and business requirements will go a long way in achieving this balance.

Throughout your duties, you will be faced with several different types of information. Some types of information are more important than others. For example, your company's trade secrets are probably more important than information about what holidays your company observes. Some information is available for public consumption, like corporate operating hours. Some information is confidential, like employee salary information. The importance of the information or the confidentiality of the information will determine how strenuous the methods used to protect the information is. Some protection methods can be very costly, so you want to make sure that the cost does not outweigh the value of the information being protected.

Before we delve in depth into specific areas of information security, we need to go over some general security concepts that apply to all areas of information security. We'll start by talking about the general principles of information security: confidentiality, integrity, and availability. Then, we'll move to information security standards, regulations, and compliance. After that, we'll cover the triple A's of information security: Authentication, Authorization, and Accounting. Then we will cover Access Control and the different models used for controlling access.

Principles of Information Security

To better understand information security and the different aspects of information security, we need to discuss the three main information security principles. Knowledge of these three principles will help guide you through your education in information security. These three principles are often referred to as the CIA triad. The three principles of the CIA triad are Confidentiality, Integrity, and Availability. Each of these principles has its own characteristics and considerations.

Confidentiality

Confidentiality is preventing the unwanted disclosure of information. Information disclosure can be very costly, especially if this information involves intellectual property or trade secrets. These types of loses can heavily impact the success of your company.

Confidentiality can be compromised in many ways. Someone may lose his or her laptop. Someone's password may be stolen. Or someone may accidentally give information to someone who is not supposed to have access to it. As an administrator, you need to take steps to prevent these compromises from happening. They could involve using encryption, strong passwords, or user education.

Integrity

Integrity is the prevention of wanted changes to data or information. If you cannot prevent unwanted changes to your data, then the validity of the data becomes suspect. Your data is no good if you can't trust its validity. You need to ensure that data cannot be tampered with, unless the appropriate approval is granted.

Integrity can be compromised in many ways. Someone can change your data intentionally or unintentionally. You need to protect against both types of compromises. Integrity can be protected by limiting access to data or using encryption.

Availability

Availability is ensuring that your data and systems are accessible by those who need access to them. Your data and your systems are useless if they cannot be accessed. Not having access to your data or systems can be just as costly as losing your data.

Availability can be affected in two major ways. One is the result of some sort of system attack or compromise. The other is the result of some sort of natural event like a fire or earthquake. Availability can be improved through the use of load balancing and redundant systems.

Information Security Standards, Regulations, and Compliance

The information security world is based on many security standards. These security standards govern what is considered secure and what isn't. During the course of managing your environment, you will undoubtedly come across these standards. It will be very beneficial to you if you understand these standards, know who set them, and understand why they were established.

Standard-Setting Organizations

Before we can discuss information security standards, we should first make sure that you know a little bit about the organizations that set these standards. These organizations are generally worldwide organizations that set international security standards. Three of the main information security standard-setting bodies are the ISO, the NIST, and the IETF.

ISO

The ISO is the International Organization for Standardization. The ISO is one the largest worldwide standards organization. The ISO has offices all over the world, but its central headquarters are located in Geneva, Switzerland. The ISO sets standards for information security, as well as many other industries. If you want more information about the ISO, you can visit its Web site at www.iso.org.

NIST

The NIST is the National Institute of Standards and Technology. It is a government agency that was founded in 1901. It is part of the United States Department of Commerce. The NIST has two main locations in Maryland and Colorado. The NIST sets standards for all areas of technology, not just information technology. If you want more information about the NIST, you can visit its Web site at www.nist.org.

IETF

The IETF is the Internet Engineering Task Force. The IETF is an international community that sets standards for the Internet. The IETF is organized into multiple entities called working groups. Each working group has a particular topic or technology that it is responsible for. Each group also has a different charter. The groups also have different chairs and directors. The IETF has an open membership, so anyone can join and attend its regular meetings. If you want more information about the IETF, you can visit its Web site at www.ietf.org.

IANA

The IANA is the Internet Assigned Numbers Authority. The IANA is responsible for IP address allocation. The IANA will delegate administration of groups of IP addresses to smaller registration bodies. The IANA is also responsible for DNS regulations. The IANA handles the operation of the root DNS domains (.com, .net, .org, and so on). If you want more information about the Internet Assigned Numbers Authority, you can visit its Web site at www.iana.org.

Security Standards and Certifications

There are many security standards or certifications that may govern your environment. Depending on your environment and which standards may apply, you may have to set specific settings for an environment. It's important that you understand these standards and how they might affect you.

FIPS

FIPS are Federal Information Processing Standards. The FIPS were developed by the U.S. federal government through the NIST. Probably the most widely known FIPS are the *FIPS 140* series. FIPS 140 focuses on cryptography. FIPS 140 sets standards for hardware and software cryptographic modules. Cryptography providers are responsible for getting their cryptographic algorithms certified with the FIPS 140 standard.

Certain environments require the use of FIPS 140-certified algorithms. If this is the case, then you must ensure that the algorithms used in your environment also adhere to this standard. You must check with your software vendors to ensure that the applications you use adhere to the FIPS 140 standard. In addition, Microsoft systems allow you to restrict cryptographic usage to only those algorithms that apply to the FIPS 140 standard. As seen in Figure 1.1, you can use the *Local Security Policy* application on a Windows 7 system to force the use of FIPS 140 compliant algorithms.

Common Criteria and EAL

Common Criteria is an international standard for information security certification. Because Common Criteria is an international standard and not just a U.S. standard, in many

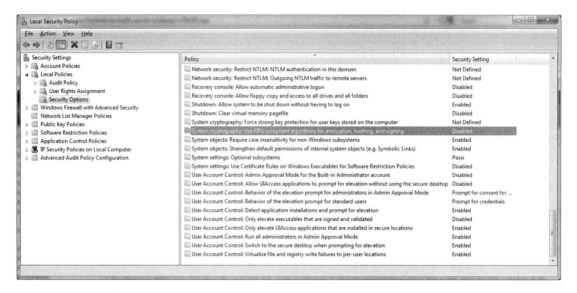

Figure 1.1 Windows 7 security policy setting for FIPS.

organizations a Common Criteria compliant environment is replacing the requirement for a FIPS 140 compliant environment.

Common Criteria provides a detailed set of requirements for certification. Common Criteria certification is achieved by hardware and software vendors. Common Criteria certification is done for a specific product or specific environment with a specific configuration. The product or environment being certified is called the Target of Evaluation (TOE). Certification of the TOE requires three components: the Protection Profile, the Security Target, and the Security Functional Requirements.

The *Protection Profile* is a document that details the secure implementation of a device or type of device. Some manufacturers use the Protection Profile as a reference when manufacturing a particular type of device. Also, the Protection Profile may feed into the Security Target used for certification.

The *Security Target* details the security configuration of the TOE. The Security Target represents the exact configuration for the certified environment. Vendors generally make the Security Target details available to their customers. This way, customers can configure their environments in a manner that reflects the certified configuration.

Security Functional Requirements are the functions that a product will provide. Common Criteria has a list of standard functions that products can provide. The functions that you want included in the evaluation must be listed.

During the Common Criteria evaluation process, you must also specify an assurance level. This is called the Evaluation Assurance Level (EAL). The EAL is an indicator of how stringent the testing is. There are seven possible EAL levels. EAL 7 is the most stringent.

Regulations and Compliance

There are different regulatory and compliance certifications that may affect your environment. Some regulations affect companies in certain industries. Some affect all companies. It's important that you understand which regulations and compliance certifications affect your organization. These rules and regulations can dramatically affect the configuration of your environment.

PCI DSS

PCI DSS is the Payment Card Industry Data Security Standard. The PCI DSS standard was established by the *Payment Card Industry Security Standards Council*. The PCI DSS standard governs systems that hold and process credit card information. The purpose is to help prevent credit card fraud and/or theft.

The PCI DSS standard has 12 requirements grouped into six categories:
- Build and maintain a secure network
  - Install and maintain a firewall configuration to protect cardholder data
  - Do not use vendor-supplied defaults for system passwords and other security parameters
- Protect cardholder data
  - Protect stored cardholder data
  - Encrypt transmission of cardholder data across open public networks
- Maintain a vulnerability management program
  - Use and regularly update antivirus software or programs
  - Develop and maintain secure systems and applications
- Implement strong access control measures
  - Restrict access to cardholder data by businesses' need to know
  - Assign a unique ID to each person with computer access
  - Restrict physical access to cardholder data
- Regularly monitor and test networks
  - Track and monitor all access to network resources and cardholder data
  - Regularly test security systems and processes
- Maintain an information security policy
  - Maintain a policy that addresses information security for employees and contractors

Adherence to the PCI DSS standard is required by the entity that is responsible for the types of credit card transactions being processed. These entities are called the acquirers. Visa, American Express, MasterCard, Discover, and other credit providers all have different acquirers. If an organization falls out of compliance, then the acquirer or body responsible for the credit card can fine the organization or cancel the organization's ability to process credit card transactions.

The PCI DSS standard calls for yearly compliance assessments. Organizations processing a smaller amount of transactions yearly can do self-assessments. Organizations processing a larger amount of yearly transactions must have their compliance assessed by a third party. This third party is called a *Qualified Security Assessor*.

SOX

SOX is the Sarbanes-Oxley Act. SOX is a government act enacted in 2002. SOX came about because of the number of corporate accounting scandals that had surfaced. The intent of SOX is to set financial guidelines for publicly traded companies. These guidelines are intended to help ensure that companies are being forthright and meeting their financial obligations to investors. The main goals of SOX are to increase transparency and force accountability.

SOX has 11 titles that define regulations for financial reporting and auditing. They are as follows:

- **Title I: Public Company Accounting Oversight Board** This title establishes an independent board to oversee auditors and auditing.
- **Title II: Auditor Independence** The purpose of this title is to prevent third-party auditors from having conflicts of interests.
- **Title III: Corporate Responsibility** This title assigns corporate executives responsibility for financial documents.
- **Title IV: Enhanced Financial Disclosures** This title establishes enhanced requirements for financial reports.
- **Title V: Analyst Conflicts of Interest** This title defines a code of conduct for financial analysts.
- **Title VI: Commission Resources and Authority** This title gives the Securities and Exchange Commission (SEC) the ability to censure securities professionals.
- **Title VII: Studies and Reports** This title requires the Comptroller General and the SEC to perform various studies related to accounting and financial reporting.
- **Title VIII: Corporate and Criminal Fraud Accountability** This title describes the penalties for altering or destroying financial records.

- **Title IX: White-Collar Crime Penalty Enhancement** This title recommends stronger sentences for white-collar crimes.
- **Title X: Corporate Tax Returns** This title says that the company CEO has to sign the company's tax return.
- **Title XI: Corporate Fraud Accountability** This title states that corporate fraud and records tampering are criminal offenses and specifies penalties for these offenses.

SAS 70

The Statement on Auditing Standards No. 70: Service Organizations (SAS 70) was developed by the American Institute of Certified Public Accountants. It's a certification done specifically for service providers. These service providers could be application service providers (ASPs), software as a service (SaaS) providers, hosted data centers, or other similar providers. There are two types of SAS 70 audits: Type I and Type II. Type I audits report on the controls that an organization has in place. Type II audits report not only on the controls that are in place but also on how these controls are being used and whether the controls are being used effectively.

SAS 70 audits are conducted by independent auditing firms. These firms investigate a company's adherence to specified security, auditing, and reporting regulations. Many companies are using SAS 70 certifications to display their compliance with other regulations like PCI or SOX. Instead of customers coming in and auditing the provider, the provider simply provides the customers with its SAS 70 certification information.

HIPAA

HIPAA is the Health Insurance Portability and Accountability Act. It was enacted by the United States Congress in 1996. HIPAA is comprised of two titles. Title I protects health insurance coverage for people who lose their jobs. Title II, which is what IT administrators care about, specifies guidelines for various healthcare agencies and institutions, including hospitals, doctors' offices, and insurance companies. The purpose of these guidelines is to ensure the privacy of patient information.

HIPAA Title II includes into five rules:
- **Privacy Rule** This rule set standards for the storage, disclosure, and distribution of confidential patient information, like medical records.
- **Transactions and Code Sets Rule** This rule sets standards around patient eligibility and filing claims.
- **Security Rule** This rule sets standards for electronic patient information.

- **Unique Identifiers Rule** This rules details the use of unique ID for healthcare providers called a National Provider Identifier (NPI).
- **Enforcement Rule** This rule set penalties for violating the HIPAA rules and regulations.

Authentication, Authorization, and Accounting (AAA)

AAA is a universally recognized acronym in the information security world. The problem is that many people are often mistaken about what the three A's are. They are Authentication, Authorization, and Accounting. Many people think they are Authentication, Authorization, and Access Control. Access control is tightly tied to authentication and authorization, but it is not part of the triple A's of information security.

Authentication

Before you give a user access to your environment, you want to first make sure you know who that user is. This is where authentication comes in. Authentication is used to verify a user's identity. Authentication can be divided into two components: identification and verification.

Before a user can be verified, the user must first be identified. Identification is the process of specifying who the user is. The identification system must have some sort of unique identifier to identify each user. This unique identifier can be in the form of a username or user ID. But it could also be a biometric identifier, an ID badge, or a smart card.

After the user has been identified, then the user must be verified. The method of verification will vary depending on the authentication system in place. If the authentication uses username and password, then the process of checking the password is considered the verification process. If the authentication system uses biometrics, then the comparison of the user biometrics against the biometric database is the verification process.

Advanced Authentication Types

Before we begin discussing different authentication methods, we should first address some advanced authentication types. The authentication methods we will discuss may make use of or be used in conjunction with these authentication types. We will cover mutual authentication, multifactor authentication, and claims-based authentication.

Mutual Authentication

Generally, in an authentication system, you can consider one system the client and another system the server. Usually, the server authenticates the client. But what about the server? How can the client be sure that the server is who it says it is? If the server's identity is not verified, then it's possible the server could be falsified. Then, the client could be submitting credentials to a malicious entity. This is where mutual authentication comes in.

In a mutual authentication scenario, both the client and the server are authenticated. The server must do something to prove its identity. This could be in the form of a server certificate or some sort of private key. Once the server has been authenticated and the client trusts the server, then the client will send its credentials to the server. This provides for a more secure authentication process and a more secure environment overall.

Multifactor Authentication

Multifactor authentication gets its name from the use of multiple authentication factors. So, what is a factor? You can think of a factor as a category of authentication. There are three authentication factors that can be used: something you know, something you have, and something you are. Something you know would be a password, a birthday or some other personal information. Something you have would be a one-time use token, a smart card or some other artifact that you might have in your physical possession. Something you are would be your biometric identity, like a fingerprint or a speech pattern. In order for something be considered multifactor authentication, it must make use of at least two of the three factors mentioned.

People often confuse two-factor authentication with dual authentication. Dual authentication is basically using any two forms of authentication in conjunction. For dual authentication, it doesn't matter if these two forms of authentication are from the same factor or not. In order for authentication to be truly two-factor, you must use authentication methods that are classified in two different factors.

Claims-Based Authentication

Claims-based authentication is a method for providing cross-platform authentication and single sign-on. A user authenticates to one authentication provider, and his or her identity is then carried over to an application or service that possibly uses a different authentication provider. It doesn't matter what the authentication providers are, as long as the different entities involved trust each other and support claims-based authentication.

Claims-based authentication is a token-based authentication system. The center of a claims-based authentication system is the Secure Token Server (STS). When a user authenticates, the STS creates a token for the user. This token contains claims about the user's identity. When the user attempts to authenticate to a claims-aware application, the application receives a token containing user claims. If the application trusts the STS that created the token, then the claims made about the user are accepted.

In some cases, the original environment and the environment the user is trying to access do not understand the same claims. In this instance, the original claims may need to be mapped to new claims. This is done through a federation trust between two token providers. One token server will read the token and claims from the other token server and will create a token that contains claims that can be used in the target environment.

Authentication Methods

There are many different authentication methods available. Each has its own advantages and disadvantages. There is no one authentication method that would work best for all environments. Authentication needs can be very environment specific. When determining which authentication method or methods should be used in your environment, you must consider not only how secure they are but also how complicated they are and the costs associated with each.

You may determine that you need different authentication methods for different users or different methods, depending on the type of resource being protected. You may also run into situations where you need to implement an application or system that doesn't support your company's standard authentication method. This actually happens quite often. In fact, most organizations have no choice but to use multiple authentication methods. If possible, you should still try to keep the same authentication source. For example, you can use native Active Directory authentication or LDAP authentication to authenticate against an Active Directory domain.

PAP

PAP is the Password Authentication Protocol. Before authentication takes place, PAP uses a handshake to establish a connection between the client and the server. After the connection has been established, the username and password are then transmitted over the connection in clear text. This clear text transmission of the username and password is one of the reasons why PAP is considered by most to be an insecure protocol. Passwords transmitted in clear text can be stolen using a basic network sniffer. So you should be careful if you choose to use PAP in your environment.

CHAP

CHAP is the Challenge Handshake Authentication Protocol. CHAP is considered more secure than PAP. CHAP uses a three-way handshake when establishing the connection. After the link is established, the server will send a challenge back to the client. The client then responds with a hashed value. The server will then check this value against the value it calculated using the hash. If the values are the same, then the connection is established. Since the hashed value is transmitted instead of the actual password, the connection process is considered more secure.

EAP

EAP is the Extensible Authentication Protocol. EAP is used in dial-up, point-to-point, and LAN connections. EAP, however, is mostly seen nowadays in wireless LAN connections. EAP is more than just a protocol; it's more of a framework. The EAP framework consists of multiple authentication methods. Some of the most commonly used ones are EAP-TLS, PEAP, and LEAP.

EAP-TLS is the Extensible Authentication Protocol–Transport Layer Security. EAP-TLS is considered very secure because of its use of client certificates. Not only is a password required for authentication, but a client certificate must also be verified. User credentials will not be passed between the client and server unless the client certificate is verified. EAP-TLS does have its potential disadvantages. The use of client certificates introduces additional complexity and cost. You can use either public certificates or private certificates. If you want to use public certificates, you have to purchase the appropriate certificates from a public certificate authority. If you choose to use private certificates, then you must figure out a way to distribute the certificate authority root certificate.

PEAP is the Protected Extensible Authentication Protocol. PEAP was developed jointly by Cisco, Microsoft, and RSA. It is used for authentication on wired and wireless networks. PEAP uses a server-side public-key certificate to verify the identity of the authentication server. An encrypted connection is then created between the client and the authentication server. The user's authentication credentials are then transmitted to the server using this encrypted connection. The public-key encryption used in PEAP produces similar complexities as those introduced by EAP-TLS. Key distribution and administration can become a costly administrative task. It's important that you have a good Public-Key Infrastructure in place when using any key or certificate-based authentication mechanism.

LEAP is the Lightweight Extensible Authentication Protocol. LEAP was developed by Cisco Systems. LEAP allows for dynamic WEP keys and mutual authentication. LEAP allows for reauthentication during a single session. Each time reauthentication occurs, new WEP keys are generated. LEAP does have its disadvantages also. LEAP has been known to have problems with passwords being cracked. Also, LEAP is a Cisco-proprietary authentication method. Although the Cisco Compatible Extensions Program has allowed third-party vendors to incorporate LEAP support, you still have to worry about compatibility.

LDAP

LDAP is the Lightweight Directory Access Protocol. There are a few misconceptions when discussing LDAP in the context of authentication. LDAP is actually a protocol used for querying a directory. When LDAP is used for authentication, what actually happens is that LDAP is used to access the directory where the user credentials are stored. The application or system being authenticated against will then perform the actual authentication.

Sometimes, there are security concerns over using LDAP for communication with the directory. In order to alleviate these concerns, you can use LDAP over SSL or LDAPS. With LDAPS, LDAP communication to the directory is encrypted using SSL. With LDAPS, you have to make sure the certificate structure is in place.

Kerberos

Kerberos is a ticketing-based authentication system. It is based on the use of symmetric keys. Kerberos uses tickets to provide authentication to resources instead of passwords. These tickets help resolve the threat of password stealing via network sniffing.

To help provide a secure environment, Kerberos uses mutual authentication. In Mutual Authentication, both the server and the client must be authenticated. This helps prevent Man-in-the-Middle attacks and spoofing.

The key components in a Kerberos system are the Key Distribution Center, the Ticket-Granting Service, and the Ticket-Granting Ticket.

Key Distribution Center: The Key Distribution Center (KDC) is the center of the Kerberos process. The KDC holds a database of the keys used in the authentication process. The KDC consists of two main parts: an Authentication Service and a Ticket-Granted Service.

The Authentication Service is what authenticates the client.

The Ticket-Granting Service is what provides tickets and Ticket-Granting Tickets to the client systems. Ticket-Granting Tickets contain the client ID, the client network address, the ticket validity period, and the Ticket-Granting Server session key.

The following steps outline the Kerberos Authentication process, as shown in Figure 1.2:

1. The user enters his or her username and password at the client system.
2. The client uses a one-way hash to mask the password. This one-way hash is considered the client secret.

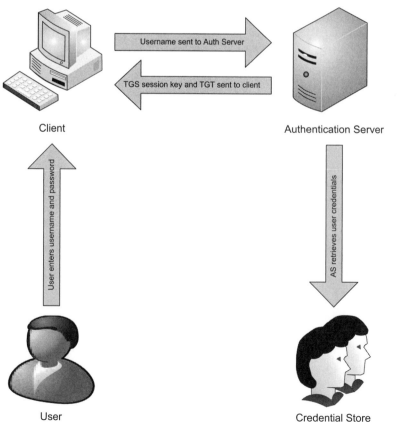

Figure 1.2 Kerberos authentication flow.

3. The client sends the username to the Authentication Server.
4. The Authentication Server retrieves the user password from the credential store and creates a one-way hash.
5. The Authentication Server checks to ensure that the client is in its approved client database.
6. If the client is approved, the Authentication Server will send back a Ticket-Granting Server session key and a Ticket-Granting Ticket.
7. The client is then authenticated to the Ticket-Granting Server.

The following steps outline the Kerberos resource request process, as shown in Figure 1.3:

1. The client sends a request to the Ticket-Granting Service. The request contains the Ticket-Granting Ticket and an authenticator encrypted using the Ticket-Granting Server session key.
2. The Ticket-Granting Service sends the client a client-to-server ticket and a client/server session key.
3. The client sends the client-to-server ticket and a new authenticator to the server where the resource resides.
4. The server then sends a confirmation message back to the client.
5. The client confirms the server and begins sending requests.

Kerberos in Windows Systems: Kerberos is very prevalent in the Windows environment. In fact, Windows 2000 and later use Kerberos as the default method of authentication. When you install your Active Directory domain, the domain controller is also the Key Distribution Center. In order to use Kerberos in a Windows environment, your client system must be a part of the

Figure 1.3 Kerberos resource access.

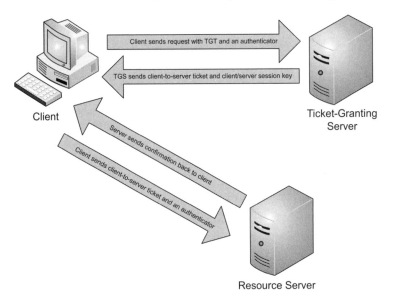

Client sends request with TGT and an authenticator

TGS sends client-to-server ticket and client/server session key

Client

Ticket-Granting Server

Server sends confirmation back to client

Client sends client-to-server ticket and an authenticator

Resource Server

Windows domain. Kerberos is used when accessing file servers, Web servers, and other network resources. When you attempt to access a Web server, Windows will try to sign you in using Kerberos. If Kerberos authentication does not work, then the system will fall back to NTLM authentication.

User Certificate-Based Authentication

Certificates can be used to perform many functions, including authentication. A certificate can be used to represent a user's digital identity. In most cases, a user certificate is mapped back to a user account. Access control will then be based on this user account.

One of the most common implementations of user certificates is via smart cards. Smart cards are plastic cards that are used to store the user certificate. When a user needs to access a system, the system will query the smart card. The user will then unlock the smart card, usually with a PIN number. After the smart card is unlocked, the certificate on the smart card is then presented to the system for authentication.

One-Time Use Tokens

One-time use tokens work by presenting the user with an alphanumeric code that must be entered into the authentication system. These codes can be generated on a hardware device, like a key fob, or via an application installed on a system. One-time use tokens are often used as part of a two-factor authentication system. In terms of authentication factor, one-time use tokens are considered "something you have."

The hardware device or application that generates the tokens is tied to a particular user. So only that user can use the codes tied to his or her key fob or application. The token codes generated by the device or application are synchronized with the authentication server. The token codes generated by token devices generally are time-sensitive; that is, the code will change after a given interval. Also, in most cases, once a code is used to authentication, it cannot be used again. You have to wait until the next code comes up before you can authenticate again. This is done to help prevent someone from stealing a code.

One-time use tokens can be expensive because of the additional cost associated with purchasing the key fobs. They are not terribly expensive, but the costs can add up in a large organization. You also have to consider the support help required for users who use one-time use tokens. Sometimes, the device becomes out of sync with the authentication server, and an administrator must resynchronize the two.

Biometrics

Biometric devices are authentication devices based on human physical or behavioral traits. Biometrics based on human physical traits generally come in the form of hardware devices like fingerprint readers, iris readers, and palm readers. Biometrics based on behavior traits often come in software form. For example, you may have a biometric software application that's based on user keystrokes. In terms of authentication factor, biometric authentication is considered "something you are."

Biometrics can be used for identification or verification. The users can enter their logon name for identification and use the biometric device for verification. Or they can simply submit their biometric identifier. The biometric system can then search its database to find a logon name associated with the users and their biometric identities. Because biometric devices require the actual user to be present for authentication, they can be a very secure method of authentication.

Biometrics can be very secure, but they can be very costly and complicated to implement. First, you have to purchase the biometric devices. Biometric devices range in price, but they can get very expensive. You also have to worry about getting all the users registered. Depending on your security model, this may mean that all users have to physically go to one central location. Someone with rights to register users would have to be posted at this location.

Open Authentication Sources

Nowadays, there are an increasing number of applications and Web sites that require authentication. Keeping track of so many different credentials can be a pretty daunting task. Because of this problem, the availability and use of open authentication sources has increased dramatically. You may remember the older Microsoft open identification source called Passport. Well, nowadays, there are several authentication sources of this type available. They include Microsoft Live ID and OpenID.

You can use these authentication sources not only for public Web sites but also in your internal corporate applications. Many open authentication vendors have SDKs and APIs available that allow companies to build their authentication mechanism into their applications. This allows you to use one authentication source for both internal and external applications. It also allows you to cut down on your administrative burden because you don't have to manage these user accounts. They are managed by the authentication provider.

Authorization

Authorization is the process of specifying what a user is allowed to do. You should have a security policy specifying what resources the users in your environment are allowed to access. You should also specify what each user is allowed to do with these resources. This security policy would be implemented using your authorization system and enforced using your access control system.

Your authorization policy should be a comprehensive as possible. In some cases, you find it necessary to delegate the creation of the authorization policy for a particular resource or application to someone who is more familiar with that resource or application. Either way, there are two concepts you may want to adhere to in order to ensure your environment is secure. These concepts are the principle of least privilege and the principle of separation of duties.

Principle of Least Privilege

The principle of least principle refers to the concept of giving a user the minimal rights needed to perform his or her job function. These help prevent users from intentionally or unintentionally doing things they shouldn't. For example, Claudine in the Accounting department should not be authorized to perform functions in the shipping system, unless using the shipping system is part of her job.

Principle of Separation of Duties

There may be an important task or process within your organization that you want to take extra precautions to protect against fraud or other misconduct. A separation of duties may help you protect this task or process. You begin by breaking the process into smaller tasks or processes. You then authorize different people to perform these smaller tasks or processes. Now, if someone wants to perpetrate a fraud, they have to enlist an accomplice who knows the other part or parts of the process. For example, if Rosa in Sales wants to get commission on a sale that actually didn't go through, she would have to convince Mary to help her because Mary signs off on all sales. Mary and Rosa would also have to convince Michelle to cooperate, because Michelle signs off on all commission checks.

Accounting

Accounting is the third A in the AAA acronym. Accounting generally goes hand in hand with auditing. Sometimes, the two are actually confused with each other. Accounting is the process of keeping track of who is accessing which resources in your environment. This information can be used for multiple purposes. You can use it to track and verify security concerns. You can also use it if you want to charge users or cost centers for system access.

AAA Protocol

Certain protocols have been developed to provide authentication, authorization, and accounting all within the same protocol. This allows you to set up one device that can support all these functions. This gives you one central place for configuration and management. These protocols are RADIUS, TACACS, and Diameter.

RADIUS

RADIUS is the Remote Authentication Dial-In User Service. RADIUS is one of the oldest AAA protocols. Originally, RADIUS was only used in remote access systems. RADIUS' uses have since expanded to include applications and network devices. RADIUS' popularity comes from the fact that it's a standard protocol that can be used on a wide variety of devices and systems.

A RADIUS setup requires a RADIUS client, a RADIUS server, and the RADIUS protocol. The RADIUS client generally exists on the device where the connection attempt is being made. That device in turn makes calls to the RADIUS server. RADIUS uses UDP for communications. By default, RADIUS uses 1812 for authentication and 1813 for accounting. Originally, RADIUS used 1645 for authentication and 1646 for accounting. You may find that some RADIUS systems still use ports 1645 and 1646.

RADIUS supports six main transaction types:
- **Access-request** The user requests access to system resources.
- **Access-accept** The user is granted access to system resources.
- **Access-reject** The user is denied access to system resources.
- **Accounting-request** This is sent to initiate the accounting process.
- **Accounting-response** This is sent if the server receives and processes the accounting-request packet.
- **Access-challenge** More information is requested from the user. This could represent a dual authentication scenario.

Microsoft Network Policy Server: Windows Server 2008 R2 comes with a built-in RADIUS implementation called Network Policy Server (NPS). NPS is installed as a server role. You can install it via Server Manager using the following procedure.

Note: This functionality was previously available through Internet Authentication Service (IAS).

1. In the Roles Summary section of Server Manager, as seen in Figure 1.4, select **Add Roles**.
2. This will bring up the Add Roles Wizard, as seen in Figure 1.5. Click **Next**.

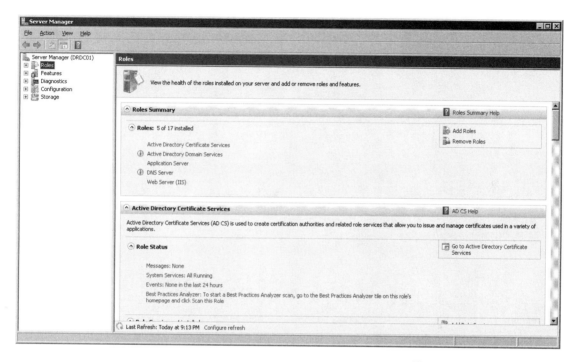

Figure 1.4 Server Manager.

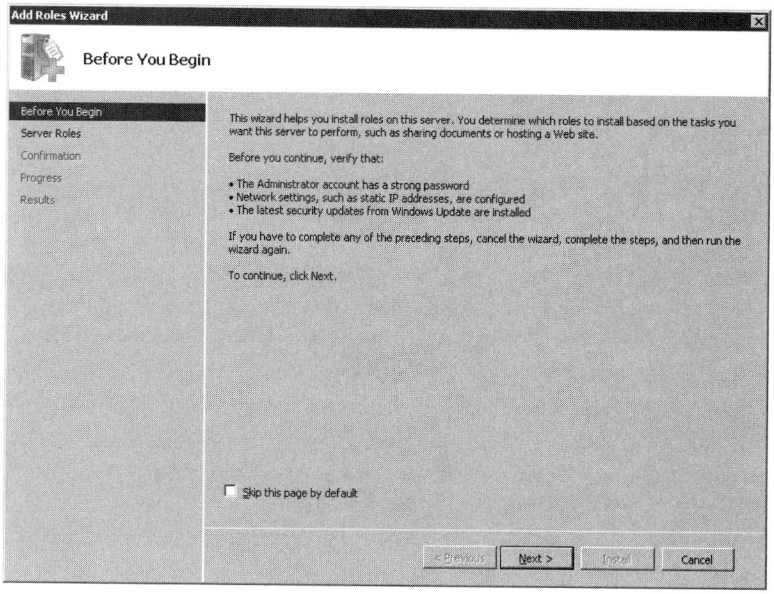

Figure 1.5 Add Roles Wizard.

3. On the Select Server Roles screen, as seen in Figure 1.6, select **Network Policy and Access Services**. Click **Next**.

4. On the Introduction to Network Policy and Access Services screen, as seen in Figure 1.7, click **Next**.

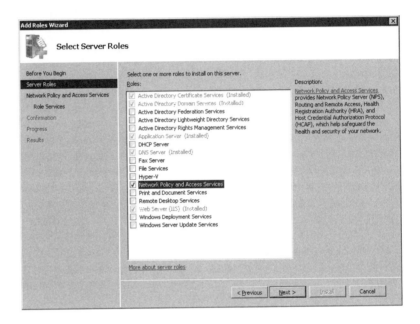

Figure 1.6 Select Server Roles screen.

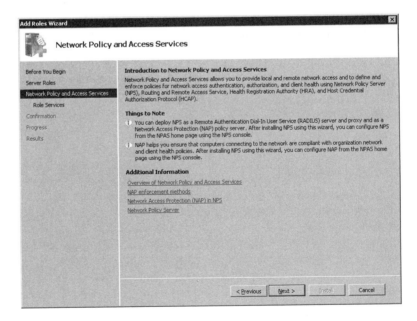

Figure 1.7 Introduction to NPAS screen.

5. On the Select Role Services screen, as seen in Figure 1.8, select **Network Policy Server**. Click **Next**.
6. On the Confirm Installation Selections screen, as seen in Figure 1.9, click **Install**.

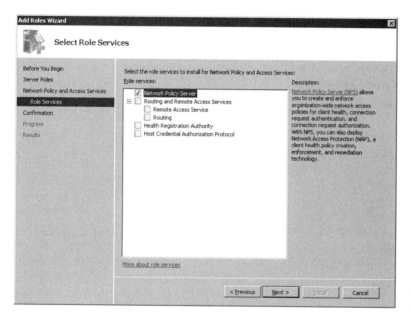

Figure 1.8 Select Role Services screen.

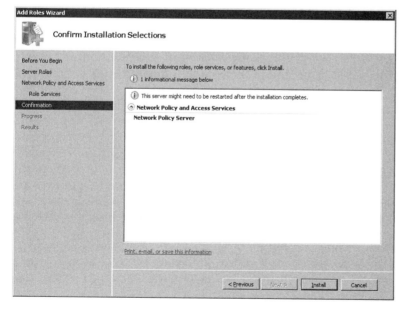

Figure 1.9 Confirm Installation Selections screen.

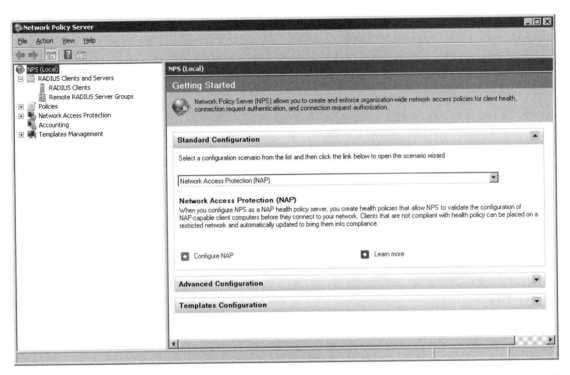

Figure 1.10 Network Policy Server.

The Network Policy Server, as seen in Figure 1.10, is accessed from the Start Menu | All Programs | Administrative Tools. Here, you can configure what systems (RADIUS clients) are allowed to use the NPS Server for authentication. You can also configure which users and groups are allowed to log in.

TACACS+

TACACS is the Terminal Access Controller Access control System. TACACS is a remote authentication standard. TACACS is used for dial-in and network access. The original TACACS standard was mostly used in UNIX systems. The original TACACS protocol is hardly used any more. It has been replaced by TACACS+ and RADIUS.

TACACS+ is a proprietary extension of the TACACS standard developed by Cisco. TACACS+ is used by Cisco for authentication users to network devices like switches, routers, and network access servers. Unlike the name suggests, TACACS+ is quite different from the original TACACS standard. In fact, they are not even compatible with each other.

TACACS is considered to be an upgrade over RADIUS. TACACS+ uses TCP for communications. TCP is considered more reliable than UDP, which is what RADIUS uses. TACACS also allows you to separate authentication and authorization into two separate processes. This allows for more flexibility in your implementation.

Diameter

Diameter is considered a successor to the RADIUS protocol. The name gives you a hint. In geometry, the diameter of a circle is twice the length of the radius of the circle. Although Diameter is considered an upgrade for RADIUS, it's important to note that RADIUS and Diameter are not directly compatible.

Diameter includes many upgrades over the RADIUS protocol. Diameter, like TACACS, uses TCP for communication, as opposed to UDP. Diameter also supports IPSec and TLS. It includes capability negotiation and error notification. Diameter also includes more attribute-value pairs.

Access Control

Authorization feeds directly into access control. Access Control systems are generally what are used to carry out your authorization policy. For example, if Carrie, Mikayla, Cori, Dakarai, and Alycia in Human Resources are the only ones authorized to view a particular set of files, then your access control system will be responsible for ensuring that only these individuals have access to the files. William, Gwen, Ruth, and Claudia, all of whom are also in the Human Resources Department, should not have access. This is the key. Just because your access control system allows someone to do something, that doesn't mean that person is authorized to do so. That could just mean there is a flaw in your access control system.

Access Control Models

Before we discuss access control models, we need to understand what access control means. Access Control is the process of determining what access users will have to a given set of resources. You have to determine which users can access the resources and what actions they can perform on the resources.

There are three main access control models used today: Mandatory Access Control, Discretionary Access Control, and Role-Based Access Control. Each has its own advantages and disadvantages. Some organizations use only one model. Some organizations use multiple models and choose to use the model that best fits a particular system or environment.

Mandatory Access Control (MAC)

Mandatory Access Control is based on hierarchical model. The hierarchy is based on security level. All users are assigned a security or clearance level. All objects are assigned a security label. Users can access only resources that correspond to a security level equal to or lower than theirs in the hierarchy.

In a MAC model, access is controlled strictly by the administrator. The administrator is the one who sets all permissions. Users cannot set permissions themselves, even if they own the object. Because of this, MAC systems are considered very secure. This is because of the centralized administration. Centralized administration makes it easier for the administrator to control who has access to what. The administrator doesn't have to worry about someone else setting permissions improperly. Because of the high-level security in MAC systems, MAC access models are often used in government systems.

There are some disadvantages to MAC systems. MAC systems can be quite cumbersome to manage. This is because the administrator must assign all permissions. Therefore, the administrator assumes the entire burden for configuration and maintenance. An administrator can quickly become overwhelmed as the systems grow larger and more complex. You must ensure that your administrative staff is resourced properly to handle the load.

Discretionary Access Control (DAC)

Discretionary Access Control is based on Access Control Lists (ACLs). The ACL lists which users have access to an object and what they can do with the object. The ACL will list users and permissions. You can give permissions or specifically deny permissions.

MAC systems use a more distributed administrative architecture. In a MAC model, access is determined by the object owner. So, if you are the owner of an object, you have full control in determining who else can access that object.

Most PC operating systems use a MAC model. Figure 1.11 shows an example from a Windows 7 system. You can see the Access Control List that is in place for one of the folders on the system.

DAC systems are generally easier to manage than MAC systems. The distrusted administrative model puts less of a burden on the administrator. The administrator is not responsible for setting the permissions on all the systems.

DAC systems can be a little less secure than MAC systems. This is in part due to the distributed management model. Since the administrator does not control all object access, it's possible that permissions can be incorrectly set, possibly leading to a breach of information. The administrator can get around this by setting up a group of systems that will be managed only by the administrator. These systems can be used to store more sensitive information.

Role-Based Access Control (RBAC)

Role-Based Access Control systems are based on a user's roles and responsibilities. Users aren't given access to systems; roles are. In an RBAC system, the roles are centrally managed by the administrator. The administrators determine what roles exist within their companies and then map these roles to job functions and tasks.

Roles can effectively be implemented using security groups. You start by creating a security group representing each role. Then, you assign permissions and rights to these groups. Next, you simply add the appropriate users to the appropriate security groups, depending on their roles or job functions.

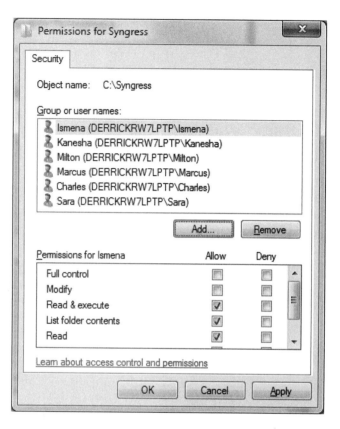

Figure 1.11 Windows 7 folder permissions window.

Because access is defined based on roles and specific job functions, you have more knowledge of what access users really require to perform this job. This information aids in being able to grant access based on the principle of least privilege. Role-Based Access models also lend themselves to making it easier to implement delegation. Delegation allows you to give administrative rights to someone else. You don't have to give them full administrative rights. You can specify certain rights for them or certain objects for them to have administrative rights over.

Role-Based Access Control systems can be difficult to implement. This is in part due to the large amount of up-front work that must be done. A lot of effort is required to identify all the various roles within an organization. It's a little easier in a newer organization. But in a large, already established organization, it can take quite some time to identify all the necessary roles and change your systems so that they recognize and make use of these roles.

Summary

Information security principles provide the basis for security standards. There are several entities and governing bodies that create standards and regulations for use with information security. Some of these rules and regulations are industry specific. But many apply no matter what the industry. It's important that you know and understand the rules and regulations that affect your organization. If not, your company could be subject to sanctions, fines, or other penalties.

A large portion of security comes down to authentication, authorization, accounting, and access control. You want to know who is accessing your environment and what is being done to it. You must take the necessary precautions and institute the necessary controls to ensure that only individuals who have authorization to have access can access the environment. If you don't have control over who is doing what, then your environment can quickly get out of hand.

CRYPTOGRAPHY

INFORMATION IN THIS CHAPTER
- Basic Cryptography Concepts
- PKI Concepts
- Implementing PKI and Certificate Management

Originally, cryptography was simply considered the process of hiding information. Nowadays, cryptography is used for much more than that. Cryptography is used for authentication, integrity, and confidentiality. One of the most common ways of implementing cryptography involves the implementation of a Public Key Infrastructure (PKI). A Public Key Infrastructure defines the processes and technologies used to implement a cryptography system. In this chapter, we'll start by discussing the key concepts needed to gain an understanding of cryptography and PKI. Then, we'll get into implementing a Public Key Infrastructure and certificate management.

Basic Cryptography Concepts

Cryptography is the center of security. Understanding the concepts involved with cryptography will help you better apply them in your day-to-day activities. We'll start by going over confidentiality and integrity and some of the different methods for implementing these concepts. Then, we'll move to cryptographic algorithms.

Confidentiality

Confidentiality corresponds with the original purpose of cryptography. Confidentiality is basically keeping your information safe or limiting the disclosure of your information. You want to

Security for Microsoft Windows System Administrators. DOI: 10.1016/B978-1-59749-594-3.00002-8

restrict information access from unwanted users. Doing this can be tricky. You want to prevent unwanted users from accessing the information, but at the same time, you don't want to make it too difficult for authorized users to access the information.

Most hackers are out to compromise the confidentiality of your systems or data. They will attempt to use your data for their own gain. In some cases, hackers will hold your data for ransom. You have to make sure you do everything you can to keep your data confidential. Depending on the type of data being lost, the consequences can be very severe. In some cases, where, for example, credit card data is lost, a company may be fined or sued if it is found that the company did not take sufficient measures to attempt to keep the data confidential. In cases like these, the issue isn't that the breach occurred; it's why the breach occurred.

There are many ways cryptography can be used to implement confidentiality. Most of these methods involve some type of encryption or hashing. Encryption and hashing scramble data so that it is not easily readable. Documents and e-mails are two forms of content that are often susceptible to loss of data confidentiality. To help secure your documents and e-mails, we will go over the use of Digital Rights Management and Pretty Good Privacy.

Digital Rights Management

Digital Rights Management (DRM) is one technology that is being used more and more to protect confidentiality. DRM is based on the concept of associating rights with documents or content. The principle is that only certain people have the rights to use certain content. It is the job of Digital Rights Management technologies to enforce these rights and ensure there are no violations.

Digital Rights Management technologies basically scramble content so that it can only be accessed by authorized parties. Only the appropriate users using the appropriate systems can descramble this content. This is the key for DRM. Not only does it have to be the appropriate user, it also has to be the appropriate system. Only that specific system knows how to unscramble the content. And the system doesn't allow anyone except authorized users access the content.

DRM is being seen all over nowadays. Many content management systems have DRM integrated into them. The systems not only store content but also perform DRM functions to prevent unauthorized access. If you store your content in one of these systems, it can only be read using the system. Even if you were able to access the content outside of the system, you would not be able to unscramble it. A lot of publicly available applications like iTunes use a form of DRM to prevent authorized accessing or sharing of content.

Pretty Good Privacy

Pretty Good Privacy (PGP) is used to ensure the confidentiality of e-mails. PGP was developed in the early 1990s. PGP encrypts the contents of e-mail messages using a combination of different methods. PGP uses hashing, data compression, symmetric encryption, and asymmetric encryption. In addition to e-mail encryption, PGP also supports the use of a digital signature to verify the sender of an e-mail.

Since its creation, PGP has kept developing and evolving. Its encryption methods have evolved, and its features have expanded. Unfortunately, PGP often doesn't support backward compatibility. So you may have trouble using different versions of PGP together. You have to make sure that both the sender and the receiver of an e-mail support the same version of PGP standard.

Integrity

Integrity is the concept of ensuring that systems and data have not been altered or changed without anyone's knowledge. Integrity pertains to only authorized changes to the systems or data. It has nothing to do with the quality or the accurateness of the data itself. Your data can have a high level of integrity, but still be incorrect. One common cryptographic means of ensuring integrity is through the use of digital signatures.

Digital Signatures

A digital signature is a digital identity that can be associated with a user. Digital signatures generally use asymmetric cryptography. Users have a private key that is only available to them. They also have a public key that is available to everyone.

Digital signatures can be used to verify someone's identity. Each user has a specific digital signature associated with them. Because of this individuality, digital signatures can be used to sign documents. Digital signatures can be used for nonrepudiation and integrity.

Nonrepudiation with Digital Signatures

Nonrepudiation is the concept of preventing someone from denying that they did something. Let's say, for example, Rudolph sent an inappropriate e-mail to Willie, Robert, and Jerry, and then later denies it. He could try to say someone else actually sent the e-mail and just used his name. Well, if the e-mail contained his digital signature, he can't deny it. It would have had to have come from Rudolph because no one else has access to his digital signature.

Integrity with Digital Signatures

Digital signatures can be used to ensure integrity. Once a document or e-mail has been signed with a digital signature, it cannot be tampered with. If someone changes the document or e-mail, the signature will be invalidated. It will have to be signed again. Unless the person tampering with the e-mail or document has a copy of a digital signature, they won't be able to re-sign it.

Using Digital Signatures with Microsoft Outlook

Microsoft Outlook allows you to use digital signatures to sign e-mails. Digital signatures are configured under the Trust Center, as seen in Figure 2.1. To access the Trust Center, from the Tools Menu, select **Trust Center**. In the left pane, select **E-mail Security**. You will see three options: Publish to GAL, Import/Export, and Get a Digital ID.

- **Publish to GAL** If available, this option will allow you to publish your default certificate to the Global Address List. This will

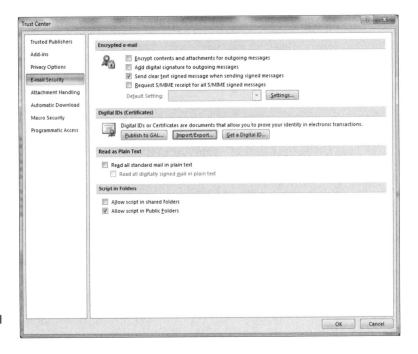

Figure 2.1 Trust Center – E-mail Security pane.

make it easier for you to exchange messages with members of your organization.

- **Import/Export** This option will bring up the Import/Export Digital ID window, as seen in Figure 2.2. From here, you can import a digital signature from a file. Or, you can export your current digital signature to a file.
- **Get a Digital ID** This option will take you to the Microsoft Web site. Here, you can get information on digital signature providers that have digital signatures compatible with Microsoft Outlook.

In the Encrypted e-mail section of Trust Center, there is an option for Encrypt contents and attachments for outgoing messages. This will apply a digital signature to all outgoing e-mails. You may not want to sign all e-mails. With Microsoft Outlook, you also have the option to attach digital signatures to specific e-mails.

Figure 2.2 Import/Export Digital ID window.

Cryptographic Algorithms

In cryptography, the strength of a transaction is based on the key. In general, the longer the key, the stronger it is. Many different systems use the same cryptographic algorithm, but they all use different keys. It's important that you keep the key safe and confidential. If the key gets lost, you will no longer be able to decrypt data that was encrypted with it. If someone else comes in possession of the key, then he or she will be able to decrypt your encrypted data.

There is a specific type of cryptographic vulnerability related to cryptographic keys. It is called weak keys. All cryptographic algorithms are based on some sort of mathematical function. Many times, mathematical functions can have numbers or series of numbers that cause the function to behave improperly. In cryptography, this number or series of numbers is called a weak key. When cryptographic algorithms are designed, the creators try to reduce or eliminate the possible number of weak keys. But, they are not always successful.

There are two general types of cryptographic ciphers: block ciphers and stream ciphers. Block ciphers encrypt data one fixed block of data at a time. The length of this block of data is called the block size. With block ciphers, the encrypted block of data will generally be the same length as the unencrypted block of data. Stream ciphers generally encrypt data one bit at a time. Stream ciphers generate and use a key stream for encryption, not just a single key. Stream ciphers are generally much faster than block ciphers. This is due to the simple mathematical formulas generally used with stream ciphers.

Symmetric Encryption

Symmetric key algorithms are sometimes referred to as secret key algorithms. This is because these types of algorithms generally use one key that is kept secret by the systems engaged in the encryption and decryption processes. This single key is used for both encryption and decryption.

Symmetric key algorithms tend to be very secure. In general, they are considered more secure than asymmetric key algorithms. There are some symmetric key algorithms that are considered virtually unbreakable. Symmetric key algorithms are also very fast. This is why they are often used in situations where there is a lot of data that needs to be encrypted.

In symmetric key algorithms, the key is shared between the two systems. This can present a problem. You have to figure out a way to get the key to all systems that will have to encrypt or decrypt data using a symmetric key algorithm. Having to manually distribute a key to all systems can be a quite cumbersome task. Sometimes, this can only be done by copying the key from a central location. You can imagine how troublesome that can be. On Windows systems, you do have the option of possibly using a group policy or a script of some kind to copy the key to the necessary systems. This helps, but the administrator is still responsible for making sure the group policy or the script functions properly.

Symmetric Key Algorithms

There are hundreds of different symmetric key algorithms available. Each has its own strengths and weaknesses. Some of the more common examples are DES, 3DES, AES, IDEA, RC4, and RC5.

DES: It is the Data Encryption Standard. DES was originally Developed in 1976. It has been one of the most widely used encryption algorithms. This is partially due to the fact that it was adopted as the government standard for encryption. The DES algorithm itself is very strong. The weakness comes in the fact that the original DES standard uses a 56-bit encryption key. Basically, you can use a computer to run through all bit combinations of the key (1s and 0s) until you hit the right key. Back when DES was originally developed, this would have taken hundreds of years. Nowadays, computers are much, much faster. In fact, nowadays, it might only take a day or so to run through all the combinations. This is the main reason why DES is no longer widely used.

3DES: It is most commonly known as Triple DES. 3DES gets its name because it applies the DES algorithm three times to each block of data. 3DES has overtaken its predecessor, DES, and is currently considered to be the most widely used standard for secure encryption. The algorithm itself is just as strong as DES, but you also have the advantage of being able to use longer key lengths. A key must be specified for each of the 3DES encryption iterations. You have the option of using the same key for each, the same for two of the iterations, or a different key for each of the iterations. The most secure implementation is to use a different key for each iteration. If you use the same key for all three iterations, the key strength is considered to be 56 bits. That's basically the same as DES. If you use the same key for two of the iterations and a different key for the third, then the key strength is considered to be 112 bits. If you use a different key for all three iterations, then the encryption strength is considered to be 168 bits. For a long time, the 3DES algorithm was the main algorithm used in FIPS 140 complaint Windows implementations. When you configured the Windows Group Policy or the registry that forced the use of FIPS 140 compliant algorithms, you were basically forcing the use of 3DES for encryption. Now, Windows systems offer the use of AES, which is also a FIPS 140 compliant algorithm.

AES: It is the Advanced Encryption Standard. It is also sometimes referred to as the Rijndael algorithm. This is due to the fact that AES actually comes from the Rijndael algorithm. The government had an evaluation process to determine which algorithm would be used as the AES standard, and the Rijndael algorithm was chosen as the winner. The AES standard actually includes three different ciphers: AES-128, AES-192, and AES-256. The numbers represent the length of the encryption key. AES is very fast and very secure. Because of this, its global uptake has been very quick.

IDEA: It is the International Data Encryption Algorithm. IDEA was originally meant to be a replacement for the DES standard. IDEA uses a 128-bit encryption key. There are two main reasons IDEA is not as widely used as planned. The first is the fact that IDEA is subject to a range of weak keys. The second reason is that there are currently faster algorithms that produce the same level of security.

RC4: It is the fourth version of the Rivest Cipher. RC4 uses a variable length encryption key. This key can vary from 40 to 256

Table 2.1 Symmetric Encryption Algorithms

	Key Length	Block Size
DES	56 bits	64 bits
3DES	56, 112, or 168 bits	64 bits
AES	128, 192, or 256 bits	128 bits
IDEA	128 bits	64 bits
RC4	40 to 256 bits	Stream cipher
RC5	0 to 2040 bits (128 recommended)	32, 64, or 128 bits (64 recommended)

bits. It's most commonly used with a 128-bit key. The RC4 algorithm is very simple and easy to implement. The problem is that if implemented improperly, it can lead to weak cryptographic systems. This is one of the main reasons why RC4 is slowly being phased out. RC4 has been one of the mostly widely used encryption algorithms. It is used in WEP and WPA on wireless networks. It has also been used in Secure Sockets Layer (SSL) and Transport Layer Security (TLS) with the Hypertext Transfer Protocol over SSL (HTTPS) protocol. RC4 has also been used with secure shell, Kerberos, and the Remote Desktop Protocol.

RC5: It is the fifth version of the Rivest Cipher. RC5 uses variable length encryption keys. They can range up to 2040 bits. The suggested key size is 128 bits. At one point, RSA, which owns the patent for RC5, was so sure of its security that it had a bounty system to reward anyone who could break items encrypted with the algorithm. Table 2.1 lists out the key length and block size for these algorithms.

Asymmetric Encryption

Asymmetric encryption is also referred to as public key encryption. In asymmetric encryption, both the encrypting and decrypting systems have a set of keys. One is called the public key, and another is called the private key. If the message is encrypted with one key in the pair, the message can be decrypted only with the other key in the pair.

Asymmetric key algorithms are not quite as fast as symmetric key algorithms. This is partially due to the fact that asymmetric key algorithms are generally more complex, using a more sophisticated set of functions.

Asymmetric Key Algorithms

Asymmetric key algorithms aren't as widely used as their symmetric counterparts. So we'll just go over two of the big ones: Diffie-Hellman and RSA.

Diffie-Hellman: The Diffie-Hellman algorithm was one of the earliest known asymmetric key implementations. The Diffie-Hellman algorithm is mostly used for key exchange. Although symmetric key algorithms are fast and secure, key exchange is always a problem. You have to figure out a way to get the private key to all systems. The Diffie-Hellman algorithm helps with this. The Diffie-Hellman algorithm will be used to establish a secure communication channel. This channel is used by the systems to exchange a private key. This private key is then used to do symmetric encryption between the two systems.

RSA: It is the Rivest Shamir Adelman algorithm. RSA was developed in 1978. RSA was the first widely used asymmetric algorithms used for signing and encryption. It supports key lengths of 768 and 1,024 bits. The RSA algorithm uses a three-part process. The first part is key generation. The keys used in the RSA algorithm are generated using mathematical operations based on prime numbers. The second part of the process is encryption. This encryption is done using one of the keys in the key pair. The third part of the process is decryption. The decryption is done using the other key in the key pair.

Hashing

Cryptographic hashing algorithms, also known as hash functions, basically scramble data. A hash function will generally take an arbitrary amount of data, apply a mathematical formula, and produce a fixed length product, called the hash value. Sometimes, you will also hear the original data referred to as the message, and the product is referred to as the message digest. Hashing is mostly used as a secure way of storing data.

Hashing relies on a couple of key principles. The first is the fact that hashes are one-way; that is, you can use the hash and the data to create the hash value, but you cannot figure out the data given the hash value. Hash functions should also avoid collisions. A collision is where two different sets of data produce the same hash value. Third, you should not be able to change data without having the hash value also change.

Hybrid Encryption Systems

There are many systems that make use of both symmetric and asymmetric keys. These are called hybrid encryption systems. These systems often make use of a key exchange protocol like the Diffie-Hellman algorithm. In these systems, an asymmetric algorithm is used to establish a connection. Then, a key is transferred between the two systems. This key is then used for establishing symmetric encryption between the two systems.

Hashing Algorithms

Hashing algorithms are just as abundant as encryption algorithms, but there are a few that are used more often than others. Some common hashing algorithms include MD5, SHA-1, SHA-2, NTLM, and LANMAN.

MD5: This is the fifth version of the Message Digest algorithm. MD5 creates 128-bit outputs. MD5 was a very commonly used hashing algorithm. That was until weaknesses in the algorithm started to surface. Most of these weaknesses manifested themselves as collisions. Because of this, MD5 began to be phased out.

SHA-1: This is the second version of the Secure Hash Algorithm standard, SHA-0 being the first. SHA-1 creates 160-bit outputs. SHA-1 is one of the main algorithms that began to replace MD5, after vulnerabilities were found. SHA-1 gained widespread use and acceptance. SHA-1 was actually designated as a FIPS 140 compliant hashing algorithm.

SHA-2: This is actually a suite of hashing algorithms. The suite contains SHA-224, SHA-256, SHA-384, and SHA-512. Each algorithm is represented by the length of its output. SHA-2 algorithms are more secure than SHA-1 algorithms, but SHA-2 has not gained widespread use.

LANMAN: Microsoft LANMAN is the Microsoft LAN Manager hashing algorithm. LANMAN was used by legacy Windows systems to store passwords. LANMAN used DES algorithms to create the hash. The problem is that LANMAN's implementation of the DES algorithm isn't very secure, and therefore, LANMAN is susceptible to brute force attacks. LANMAN password hashes can actually be cracked in just a few hours. Microsoft no longer uses LANMAN as the default storage mechanism. It is available, but is no longer turned on by default.

NTLM: This is the NT LAN Manager algorithm. The NTLM algorithm is used for password hashing during authentication. It is the successor of the LANMAN algorithm. NTLM was followed with NTLMv2. NTLMv2 uses an HMAC-MD5 algorithm for hashing.

PKI Concepts

PKI is a Public Key Infrastructure. As the name suggests, it is based on the use of public, or asymmetric, key encryption. PKI allows you to engage in secure transactions on insecure networks. The most common of these insecure networks is the Internet. PKI generally manifests itself through the use of digital certificates. Digital certificates are used to map keys to users and systems.

Certificate Authority

The Certificate Authority (CA) is the center of the certificate process. The Certificate Authority is the entity that actually issues the digital certificate. The digital certificate contains a public key and the identity of the owner. The CA is considered to be the link between these two. When a system accesses another system that uses a certificate, the originating system will use the Certificate Authority to verify the identity of the target system and the information contained within the certificate.

Certificate Authority Trust Model

The Certificate Authority trust model outlines how your Certificate Authorities will be organized. If you are deploying an internal Certificate Authority, it's important that you take the time to choose the model that will best fit your needs. Each has its own advantages and disadvantages. There are three trust models that can be used: the Single CA model, the Hierarchical CA model, and the cross-certification model.

Single CA Model

The Single CA model uses only one Certificate Authority. All certificate requests will be processed by that CA. The Single CA model works well in smaller organizations, but larger organizations generally benefit from using a different model.

Having a Single CA makes it easy to administer. There is only one system you have to worry about. The Single CA model can also be very secure. You have to secure only one system. You also have more control over what certificate requests are processed.

The Single CA model does have its disadvantages. First, it doesn't scale very well. All requests have to go to a single system. This system can become busy processing requests. Having a Single CA also represents a possible single point of failure. If that one system fails, certificate transactions cannot be processed.

Hierarchical CA Model

In a Hierarchical CA model, there are multiple Certificate Authorities. The Root CA will authorize other CAs, called Subordinate CAs to process certificate transactions. The Root CA is still considered the start of authority for the CA system. The Subordinate CAs are the ones that do most of the work. The Subordinate CAs can be either Intermediate CAs or Issuing CAs. Intermediate CAs can issue certificates only to Subordinate CAs. Issuing CAs can issue certificates to users and client devices. Figure 2.3 shows a sample CA hierarchy.

A Hierarchical CA model is much more scalable than the Single CA model. In the hierarchical model, you have multiple systems

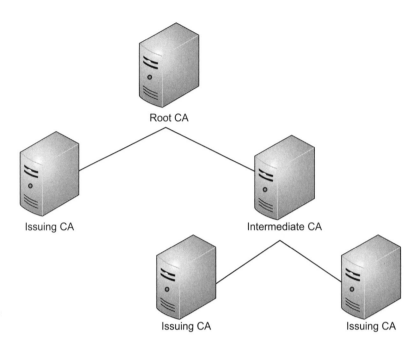

Figure 2.3 Certificate Authority hierarchy.

processing certificate requests. If you need to add capacity, you can simply add an additional Subordinate CA.

A Hierarchical CA model also requires more administrative effort. You now have to administer not only the Root CA but also the Subordinate CAs. Also, since there are more systems to deal with in a hierarchical model, security is a bigger concern. You have to make sure that you secure multiple systems, not just one like in the Single CA model. One security measure that is sometimes used is to take the Root CA offline. This prevents people from being able to access it directly. If the Root CA were compromised, all the CAs in the hierarchy would be invalidated.

How Clients Trust CAs

When you receive a certificate during a transaction, that certificate basically links an identity with a key pair. You trust that the identity specified in that certificate is actually the appropriate and expected owner of the key pair. How do you know that the certificate is correct? There is no real way for you to know. Basically, you are trusting that the Certificate Authority that issued the certificate did what it needed to do, in order to verify the identity. Being that anyone can create a Certificate Authority, you can assume that some CAs are more trustworthy than others.

So, how does your system know that you trust a particular Certificate Authority? This is done by adding the certificate for the Certificate Authority to your list of trusted Root CAs. By default, Windows comes with many preinstalled root certificates. But there may be instances where you need to add one, like in the case of a private Certificate Authority.

Certificates can be added to a user store, in which case they will be available only to that user. They can be added to a service store, in which case they will be available only to that service. Or they can be added to the local machine store, in which case they will be available to the whole system.

Adding a Certificate to the Local Machine Store

1. Open an MMC console.
2. Select **File | Add/Remove Snap-in**.
3. In the Available snap-ins section of the Add or Remove Snap-ins window, as seen in Figure 2.4, select the **Certificates snap-in**. Click **Add**.
4. The Certificates snap-in window will appear. Select **Computer account** and click **Next**.
5. In the Select Computer window, select **Local Computer**. Click **Finish**.
6. Now you are back at the Add or Remove Snap-ins window. Click **OK**.
7. If you expand Certificates (Local Computer) | Trusted Root Certification Authorities | Certificates, you will be able to see all the trusted root certificates available to the system.
8. To add an additional root certificate, right-click the Certificates folder and select **All Tasks | Import**.

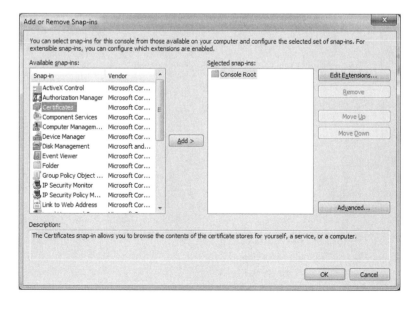

Figure 2.4 Add or Remove Snap-in window.

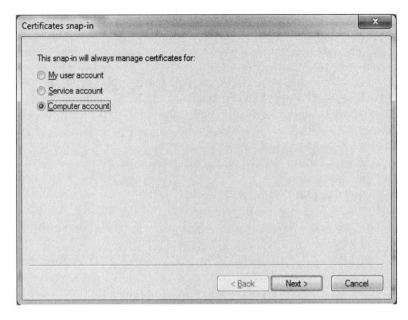

Figure 2.5 Certificates Snap-in window.

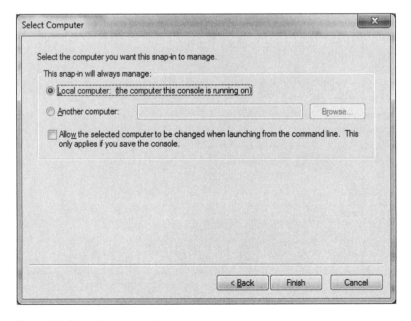

Figure 2.6 Select Computer window.

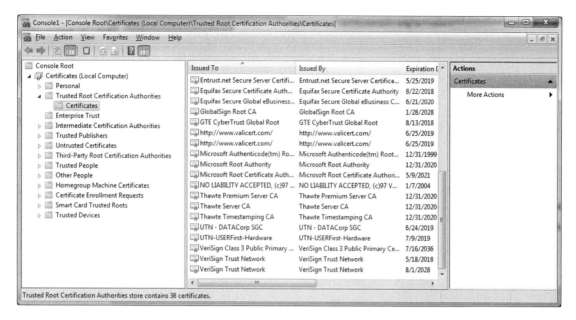

Certificate Path

Often, there are multiple certificate authorities between the Root
CA and the user or system that a certificate was issued to. There
could be several Intermediate CAs or Issuing CAs in the list. This
list of entities is called the certificate path. The certificate path
describes how a certificate maps back to the root. If any entity in
the certificate path is not trusted, then the certificate itself may
not be trusted.

Certificate Trust List

A certificate trust list (CTL) is a predefined list of trusted entities. A CTL may contain a list of certificates and a list of acceptable uses. You can use a CTL to ensure a system will trust a
certain certificate it may receive. You can also specify what certain certificates can be used for, like digital signatures or server
authentication.

Key Management

Keys are the most important part of the cryptography structure.
It's important that these keys are properly taken care of. You must
first determine what type of key management model you will

use. Then, you need to determine how you will handle different aspects of key management, such as storage, expiration, suspension, recovery, renewal, and destruction.

Storage

Proper key storage is essential. If your keys become compromised, then they are considered worthless. What point is there in encrypting something if the key that can be used to unencrypt it is available to anyone? In cases of public key encryption, it's especially import to secure the private key. The public key is already available to anyone, but the private key is not.

Hardware versus Software Storage

You have two general options for key storage. You can use a hardware method or a software method. Hardware key storage is generally more expensive, but it is also considered more secure. With hardware key storage, there is a specialized hardware module designed specifically for storing keys. In some cases, the hardware module will also process the cryptographic transactions for you. However, hardware modules usually just perform key storage, so all their resources are committed to this.

Software key storage is generally lower in cost and easier to manage. In software key storage, an application of some sort is responsible for the key storage. The system itself doesn't have to be specialized and may even perform a myriad of other functions.

Escrow

Escrowing is the process of backing up the public and the private key together. This is done for recovery purposes. If something happens to a certificate, you can retrieve the public and private key and use them to re-create the certificate. When you escrow, you should make sure you secure the location where the keys will be kept. Protection of the private key is especially important.

Table 2.2 Hardware Key Storage vs. Software Key Storage

	Cost	Security	Ease of Management
Hardware storage	More expensive	More secure	More difficult to manage
Software storage	Less expensive	Less secure	Easier to manage

Expiration

After the validity period for a certificate has past, the certificate expires. After a certificate has expired, it can no longer be used. Any systems attempting to use an expired certificate or clients attempting to access a system with an expired certificate will at the very least receive a warning message. In some cases, connection attempts may be denied. To prevent this scenario, you are encouraged to renew your certificates well before they expire.

The expiration of the root certificate for a Certificate Authority can be an especially troublesome situation. When the root certificate for a Certificate Authority expires, then the trust can no longer be established between clients and the certificates that were issued by that Certificate Authority. At that point, all the certificates issued by that Certificate Authority are virtually worthless. You will need to notify the owners of the systems with the problem certificates that the Certificate Authority root certificate has expired and that they will need to request new certificates. You can help avoid this problem by carefully monitoring the expiration of the root certificate and tailor your certificate distribution accordingly.

Suspension

The suspension process temporarily suspends the use of a certificate. If you suspect there is a problem with a certificate, you can suspend usage while you conduct an evaluation. The key here is that certificate suspension is temporary. After your investigation is completed, and you are satisfied with the result, you can resume use of the certification. Neither the certificate nor the keys have to be regenerated.

Revocation

The process of revocation renders a certificate invalid, meaning the certificate can no longer be used. A key point to note is that revocation is permanent. Once a certificate has been revoked, it generally cannot be reinstated. As such, you want to revoke a certificate only where absolutely necessary. There are many reasons why a certificate can be revoked. These include the private key being compromised, the certificate being improperly obtained, the CA being compromised, or the information in the certificate no longer being valid.

A certificate is associated with a public key and a private key. You should take caution to ensure that the private key is secure. Anyone who is in possession of the private key can use it to decrypt messages meant for the system. Sometimes, you cannot avoid loss of the private key. A system where the private key is stored may be compromised. Or you may have to terminate an employee who had access to the private key. If Abigail, who was on the team that managed a particular server, was terminated, you may not be able to ensure that she didn't take a copy of the private key with her. Depending on the server and the information it contains, you may not want to take a chance that Abigail won't do something malicious, so you may want to revoke the certificate for that server and issue a new one.

Even though great care is generally used when issuing certificates, there are circumstances where a certificate can be improperly obtained. This could be the result of some malicious act or an accident. Patricia from Human Resources, who doesn't request certificates often, may not have entered all the appropriate information when she requested a certificate. This may result in your having to invalidate the certificate and revoke it. You may also get someone who intentionally tries to register a certificate for a server or domain he or she does not have control over. This may be done in an attempt to conduct some sort of spoofing attack.

It barely ever happens, but there can be a case where the Certificate Authority is compromised. If the Certificate Authority is compromised, then all the certificates issued by that Certificate Authority are considered compromised. In this case, you must revoke all the certificates issues by that CA. They will then all have to be reissued. This is one of the most extreme cases.

The most common situation where a certificate would have to be revoked is where information in the certificate has changed. This could be caused by a merger, an acquisition, or the transfer or change of a DNS name. In this case, the old certificate would be revoked, and a new certificate would be issued with updated information.

Status Checking

Revoking or suspending a certificate does no good unless others know about it. Unless a system knows that a certificate has been revoked or suspended, the system will continue to trust that certificate. To help with the notification process, you can use a couple of options. The first is a Certificate Revocation List (CRL). The second is the use of the Online Certificate Status Protocol (OCSP).

A CRL will list all the certificates that have been either suspended or revoked. CRLs are published by Certificate Authorities. Generally, the root certificate for a Certificate Authority will specify the location of that CA's CRL. If a system is configured properly, it will check CRLs to ensure the validity of certificates. This check can happen when a certificate is accessed or on a periodic basis. Many systems can keep locally cached copies of the CRLs it checks. This keeps the system from having to check a remote CRL every time it needs to access a system that uses a certificate.

To assist in the process of CRL checking, the concept of delta CRLs was developed. CRLs can become quite large. So downloading an entire CRL can consume a lot of bandwidth. This is especially troublesome because, in most cases, they will be downloaded over a bandwidth-limited Internet connection. With delta CRLs, clients do not always have to download an entire CRL. Delta CRLs are CRLs that include only CRL changes since the last full CRL was published. So if clients have the latest full CRL, they will need to download only the latest delta CRL to have the most current list.

Configuring Internet Explorer for CRL Checking

1. In Internet Explorer, go to Tools | Internet Options.
2. Go to the Advanced tab.
3. Under the Security section, check the box for Check for server certificate revocation. You will be required to restart Internet Explorer before this will take effect.

   Note: There is also an option for Check for publisher's certificate revocation. This option will enable CRL checking for online software publishers.

Configuring Firefox for CRL Checking

There are two ways to add CRL checking to Firefox: the manual way and the more automated way. We will start with the more automated way.

1. Navigate to the URL of the server that contains the CRL.
2. Click the link for the CRL.
3. The CRL will be imported, and you will be presented with the CRL Import Status window, as seen in Figure 2.9. Click **Yes** to enable automatic updating of the CRL.
4. You will then see the Automatic CRL Update Preferences window. Click the box for Enable Automatic Update for this CRL. Click **OK**.

   Now, we will go through the more manual process.

1. Inside Firefox, go to Tools | Options.
2. Go to the Encryption tab, under the Advanced menu.

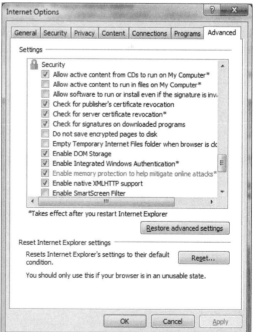

Figure 2.8 Internet Explorer CRL checking.

Figure 2.9 Firewall CRL Import Status window.

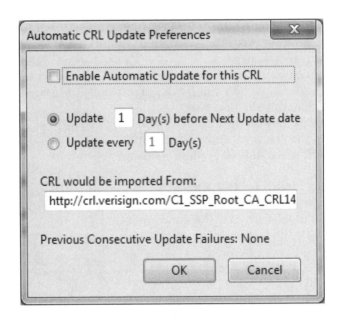

Figure 2.10 Firefox Automatic CRL Update Preferences window.

3. In the Certificates section, select the option for Revocation Lists. This brings up the Manage CRLs window, as seen in Figure 2.11. Click **Import**.
4. In the Import Certificate Revocation List window, enter the URL for the CRL you would like to import. Click **OK**.
5. The CRL Import Status will appear. Click **Yes** to configure automatic updating of the CRL.
6. Click the box for Enable Automatic Update for this CRL. Click **OK**.
7. You can now close the Manage CRLs window.

Figure 2.11 Firefox Manage CRLs window.

Figure 2.12 Firefox Import Certificate Revocation List window.

The Online Certificate Status Protocol created an alternative to using Certificate Revocation Lists. OCSP is useful because the client only requests and receives information about a specific certificate. It doesn't have to process an entire CRL. When a client wants to verify a certificate, it will send an OCSP request to an OCSP server. The OCSP server will respond with a signed OCSP response. The client will then verify the response. If the response can be validated, then the client will process the information inside the response. You can also configure systems to check an OCSP server to check for certificate validity.

Configuring Firefox for OCSP

1. Inside Firefox, go to Tools | Options.
2. Go to the Encryption tab of the Advanced menu.
3. In the Certificates section, select the option for Validation. This brings up the Certificate Validation window, as seen in Figure 2.13.
4. Click the box for Use OCSP. Click **OK**.

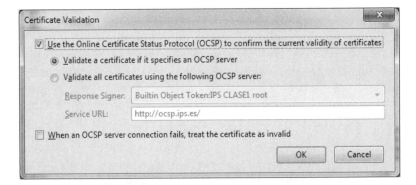

Figure 2.13 Certificate Validation window.

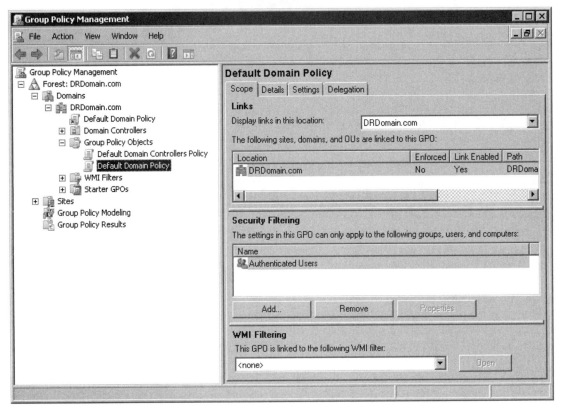

Figure 2.14 Group Policy Management application.

Configuring Certificate Revocation Checking via a Group Policy

Certificate revocation checking can be configured in the browser or for the entire operating system. Configuring revocation for the operating system allows the settings to apply no matter what method is used for communications.

1. Open the Group Policy Management application under Start | Administrative Programs.

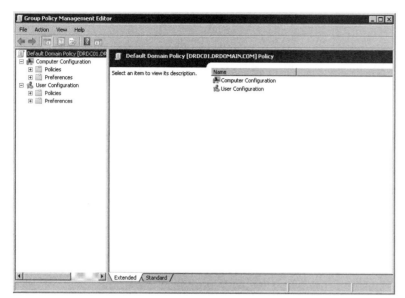

Figure 2.15 Group Policy Management Editor.

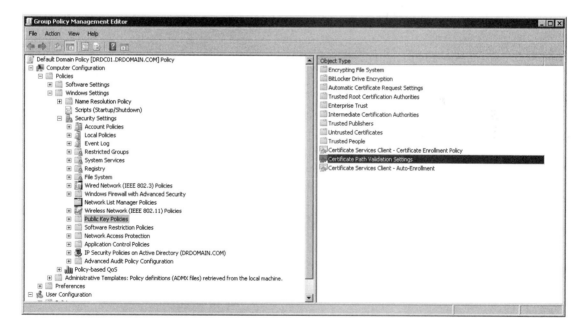

Figure 2.16 Public Key Policies.

2. Under Group Policy Objects, right-click the Default Domain Policy and select **Edit**. This brings up the Group Policy Management Editor.
3. Double-click on Certificate Path Validation Settings under Computer Configuration | Policies | Windows Settings | Security

Settings | Public Key Policies. This brings up the Certificate Path Validation Settings Properties window.

4. On the Revocation tab, check the option for Define these policy settings. You can now configure your CRL and OCSP settings.

Recovery

A recovery is performed when a certificate needs to be restored. This could be because the certificate was lost or has become corrupted. During the recovery process, the public and private keys are restored from backup. These keys are then used to re-create the certificate.

Renewal

Certificates are generally not valid forever. They have a validity period. If you want to continue to use a certificate, it should be renewed before the validity period ends. To renew a certificate, a request is made to the Certificate Authority. Once the Certificate Authority verifies the identity of the requester, a new certificate is generated.

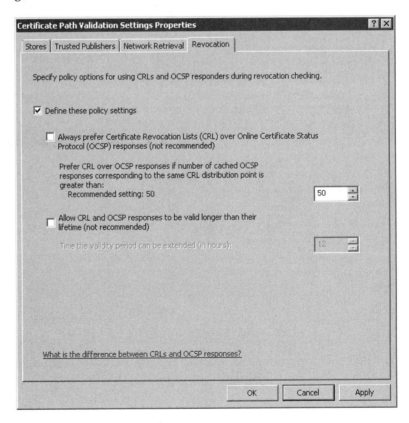

Figure 2.17 Public Key Policies – Revocation tab.

Tools & Traps

Digital Certificates and Time

Time is very important when dealing with digital certificates. If two systems are trying to establish a secure connection, differences in system time can become an issue. Depending on the configuration, two systems may not be able to be connected if the disparity in time between them passes a certain threshold. One mistake sometimes made when using certificates is attempting to use a certificate before the validity period starts. If the time on your Certificate Authority and the time on the system requesting the certificate are not in sync, you could run into a situation where the validity period for the certificate has not started. These issues do not happen often, but they are possible. One way to eliminate this risk is to ensure that the time on all your systems is in sync. This can be done through the use of a centralized time server.

Destruction

When certificates and the keys associated with them are no longer being used, the certificate should be destroyed. This would prevent anyone from being tempted to use the certificate. After a certificate is destroyed, it should be added to the Certificate Authority's CRL. This will help notify clients that the certificate is no longer valid. When a certificate is destroyed, it is a good idea to archive the private key first. This is done just in case a situation arises where you might need to use it later.

Implementing PKI and Certificate Management

It's important that the proper level of planning go into implementing your Public Key Infrastructure. You start by becoming familiar with all the concepts surrounding PKI. Next, you put together your plan for implementing PKI within your organization. Finally, you build your PKI. We are going to go through some of the applications and tools that you will use to build and maintain your PKI.

Active Directory Certificate Service

Microsoft's implementation of a PKI is done through the use of Active Directory Certificate Services. Active Directory Certificate Services is a role that can be added to your Windows Server 2008 R2 system. When you are installing Active Directory Certificate Services, there are several role services that you can choose. It's important that you understand what they are and what they do before you start your installation.

- **Certificate Authority** This will install a CA that can be used to process certificate requests.
- **Certificate Authority Web Enrollment** This will create a Web site front end for your CA that users can use to request certificates.
- **Online Responder** This will allow you to configure your server to be an Online Certificate Status Protocol responder.
- **Network Device Enrollment Service** This will allow you to issue certificates for network devices, such as routers and switches. The Certificate Authority services must be set up before this service can be installed. They cannot be installed simultaneously.
- **Certificate Enrollment Web Service** This allows a nondomain computer to request certificates. The Certificate Authority services must be set up before this service can be installed. They cannot be installed simultaneously.
- **Certificate Enrollment Policy Web Service** This allows computers to receive Certificate Enrollment Policy information.

Installation of Active Directory Certificate Services

1. Open Server Manager
2. In the Roles Summary section, select the option for **Add Roles**.
3. This brings up the Add Roles Wizard. Click **Next**.
4. On the Select Server Roles window, select **Active Directory Certificate Services**. Click **Next**.
5. This brings up the Introduction to Active Directory Certificate Services window. Here, you will receive a warning about changing the name or domain of the computer. Click **Next**.

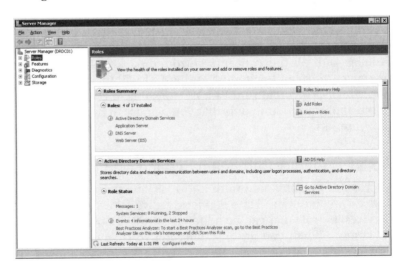

Figure 2.18 Windows Server 2008 R2 Server Manager.

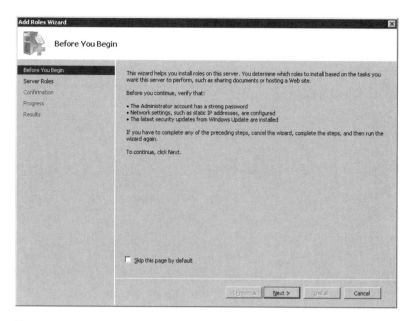

Figure 2.19 Add Roles Wizard.

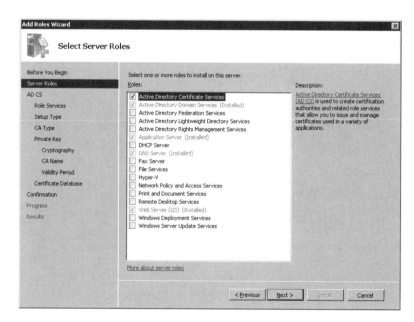

Figure 2.20 Add Roles Wizard – Server Roles screen.

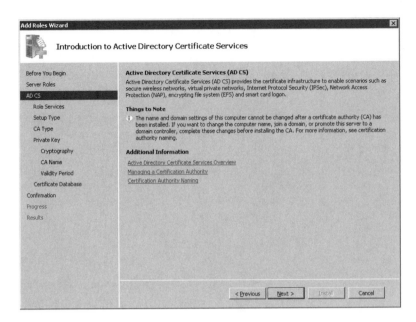

Figure 2.21 Add Roles Wizard – Introduction to Active Directory Certificate Services.

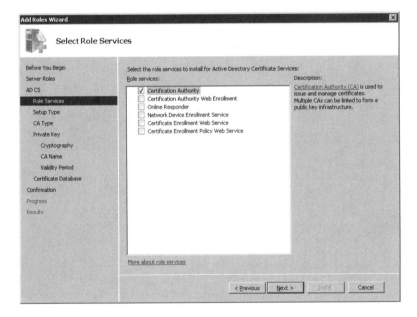

Figure 2.22 Add Roles Wizard – Select Roles screen.

6. This brings up the Select Role Services window. Select the roles you would like to add.

7. This brings up the Setup Type screen. Here, you specify whether you want to install an Enterprise CA or a Standalone CA. We will install an Enterprise CA. Click **Next**.

8. On the Specify CA Type screen, you have to select whether you are installing a Root CA or a Subordinate CA. Because this will be the first CA in our Enterprise, we will choose **Root CA**. Click **Next**.

9. Now, you will be on the Set Up Private Key screen. Here, you determine whether to use an existing private key or create a new one. If you were reinstalling a CA, you would select Use existing private key. Because we are creating a new CA, we will select **Create a new private key**. Click **Next**.

10. Next is the Configure Cryptography for CA screen. Here, you select a Cryptographic Service Provider, a hashing algorithm, and a key length to be used when the CA signs certificates. We will use RSA#Microsoft Software Key Storage Provider, SHA-1, and a key length of 2048 characters. Click **Next**.

11. Now, we have the Configure CA name screen. Here, we must specify a name for the CA. By default, Windows 2008 R2 uses a combination of the machine name and the system's DNS

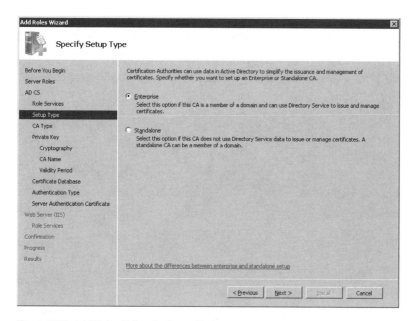

Figure 2.23 Add Roles Wizard – Setup Type screen.

suffix. You can change this if your desire. We will accept the defaults. Click **Next**.

12. Next is the Set Validity Period screen. Here, you specify how long the CA's certificate will be valid. Once its certificate expires, the CA will no longer be able to process a certificate

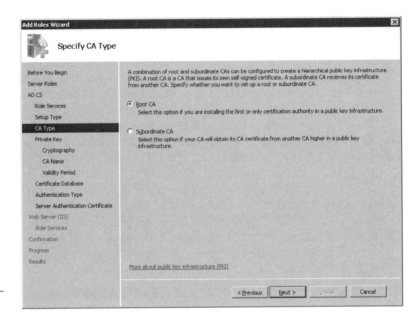

Figure 2.24 Add Roles Wizard – CA Type screen.

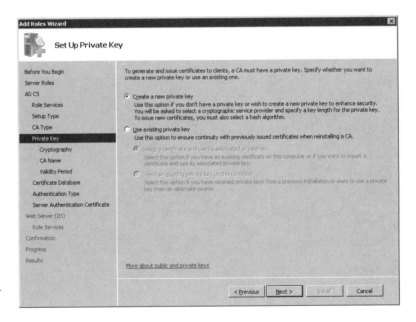

Figure 2.25 Add Roles Wizard – Set Up Private Key screen.

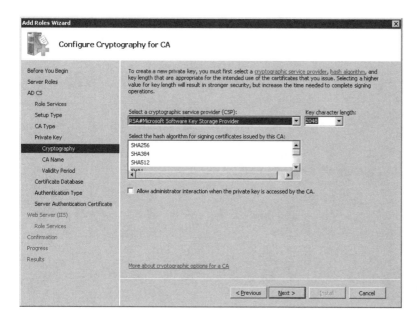

Figure 2.26 Add Roles Wizard – CA Cryptography screen.

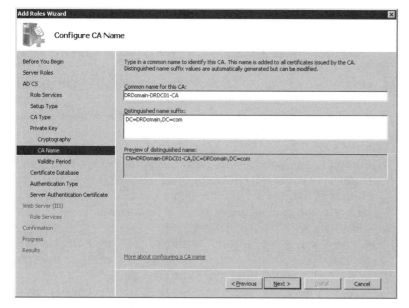

Figure 2.27 Add Roles Wizard – CA Name screen.

request. Also keep in mind that the CA will also not be able to generate certificates that would expire after the CA validity period ends. We will accept the default of five years. Click **Next**.

13. On the Configure Certificate Database screen, you must specify where the certificate database and the certificate

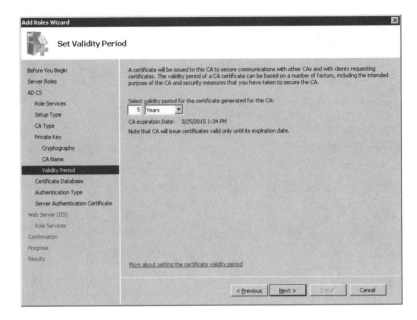

Figure 2.28 Add Roles Wizard – Validity Period screen.

database logs will be located. We will accept the default locations. Click **Next**.

14. On the Select Authentication Type screen, you can choose
what type of authentication clients must use when making
Web-based requests to the CA. We will use Windows Integrated Authentication. Click **Next**.

15. Next is the Choose Server Authentication Certificate for SSL
Encryption screen. You use this screen if you want users to
make HTTPS connections to your CA's Web site. You can
choose an already installed certificate or choose to install one
later. We will choose the option for Choose and assign a certificate for SSL later. Click **Next**.

16. As we have seen, some Certificate Service Role options
require that changes be made to IIS. The wizard will now take
us through making those changes. Click **Next**.

17. Now, you have the Select Role Services window for IIS. Here,
you can see what services are being added to the Web Server
(IIS) role. Click **Next**.

18. Finally, you reach the Confirm Installation Selections window.
Here, you can review all the installation settings you set. If
everything appears to be OK, click **Install**.

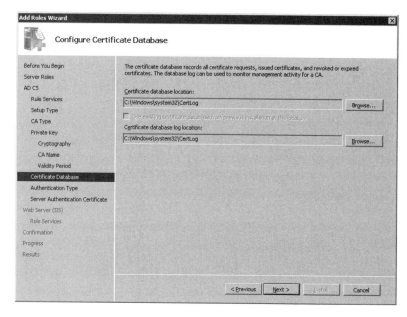

Figure 2.29 Add Roles Wizard – Certificate Database screen.

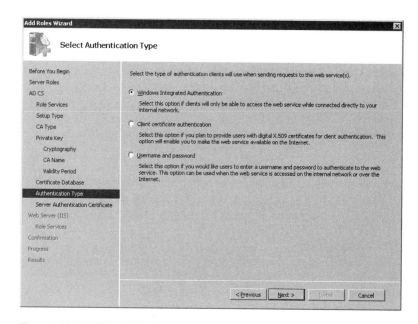

Figure 2.30 Add Roles Wizard – Authentication Type screen.

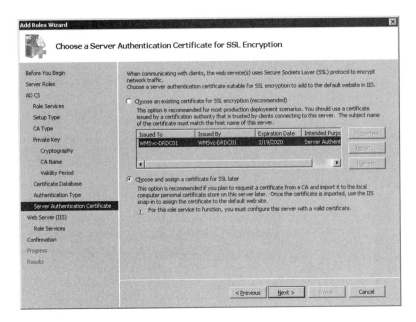

Figure 2.31 Add Roles Wizard – Server Authentication Certificate Selection screen.

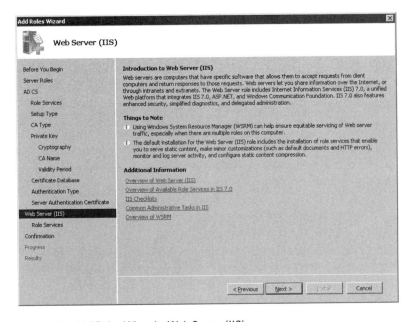

Figure 2.32 Add Roles Wizard – Web Server (IIS).

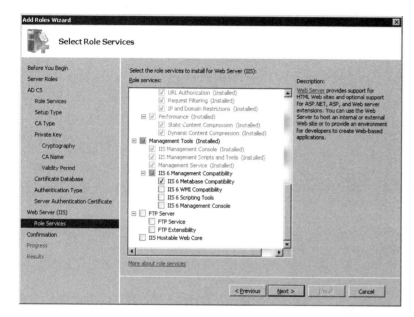

Figure 2.33 Add Roles Wizard – Web Server (IIS) – Role Services screen.

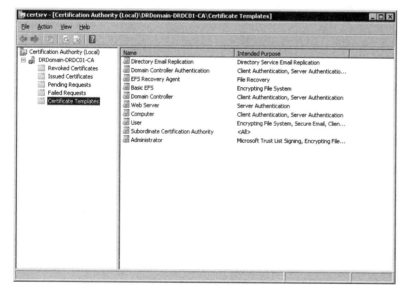

Figure 2.34 Certificate Authority MMC snap-in.

Configuration

The main place where you will go to configure and manage your Certificate Authorization is the Certification Authority MMC snap-in, as seen in Figure 2.34. In the CA MMC snap-in, you can configure your certificate policies, enable and disable certificate templates, and control who can request what certificates. You can also view and process certificate requests.

Certificate Requests

Once your Certificate Authority is up and running and you have configured which types of certificates you want it to distribute, it can begin servicing user requests. There are several ways users can request certificates. We will cover the most common, using the Certificate Authority Web Service.

Users interact with the Certificate Authority Web Service, by accessing the CA's Web site. The URL for the CA is usually https://<server_name>/certsrv. Through this Web site, users can request certificates, view the status of a pending request, download the root certificate for a CA, or download the CA's Certificate Revocation List.

Requesting a User Certificate

To request a User Certificate using the Certificate Authority's Web site, do the following:

1. In your Web browser, navigate to the Web site for the Certificate Authority.
2. Under the Select a task section, click the option for **Request a certificate**.
3. On the Request a certificate page, select the option for **User Certificate**.
4. Click **Yes** on the Web Access Confirmation window.

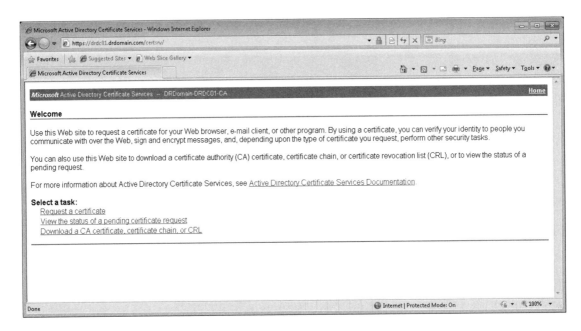

Figure 2.35 Certificate authority Web site.

5. On the User Certificate – Identifying Information page (see Figure 2.38), click **Submit**. The certificate request will be created using the name of the user that was used to log into the Certificate Authority's Web site.
6. Click **Yes** on the Web Access Confirmation window.
7. You now have the option to install the certificate. This is because your Certificate Authority is not configured to require administrator approval for the user's certificate requests. Click **Install this certificate**.

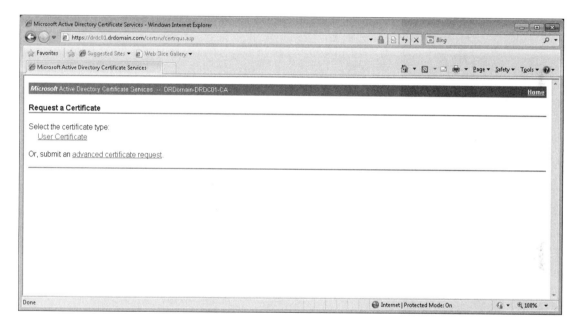

Figure 2.36 Certificate authority request a certificate page.

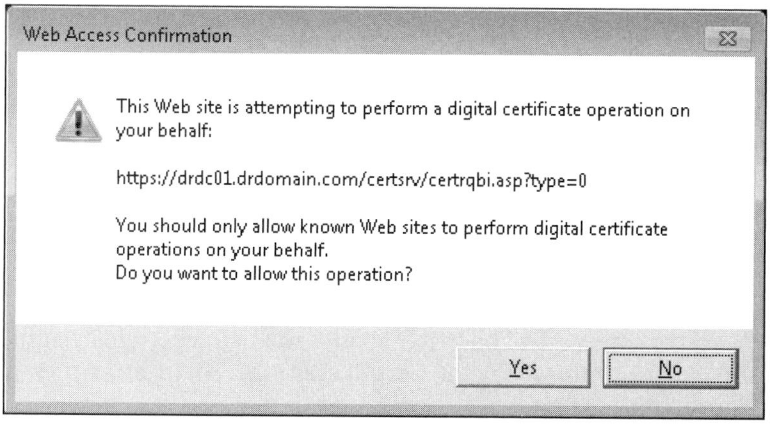

Figure 2.37 Web Access Confirmation window.

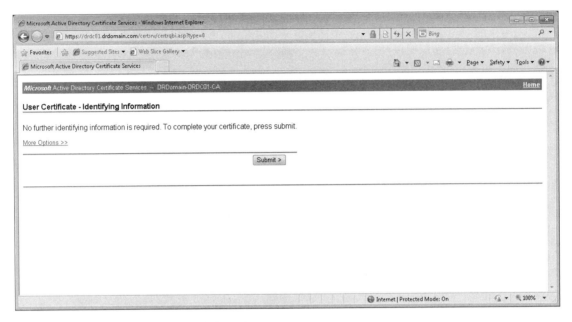

Figure 2.38 User Certificate – Identifying Information page.

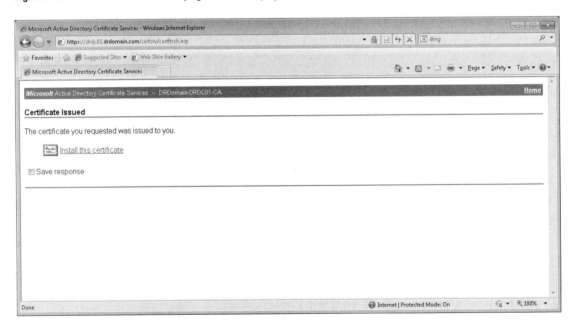

Figure 2.39 Certificate authority certificate issued page.

The certificate will be installed into the user's certificate store. You can verify this using the Certificates MMC snap-in, as seen in Figure 2.40.

Viewing the Status of a Certificate Request

If you have a pending certificate request, you can use the Certificate Authority Web Site to view the current status of your request.

To check the status of your request, do the following:

1. In your Web browser, navigate to the Web site for the Certificate Authority.
2. Click the option for **View the status of a pending certificate request**.
3. On the Certificate Request status page, select the request you want a status for.

If your request is still pending, you will see something similar to what is in Figure 2.42.

If your request was approved, you will be presented with the Certificate Issued page.

Downloading a CA's Root Certificate, Certificate Chain, or CRL

1. In your Web browser, navigate to the Web site for the Certificate Authority.
2. Click the option for **Download a CA certificate, certificate chain, or CRL**.
3. Click **Yes** on the Web Access Confirmation window.
4. On the CA Certificate Download page, you can download the CA certificate, the CA certificate chain, the latest base CRL, or the latest delta CRL. When you click one of the links, you will be prompted to either install or save the desired item.

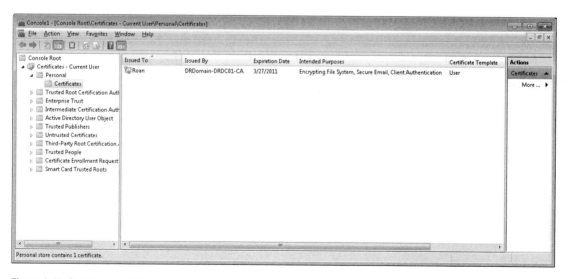

Figure 2.40 Certificates MMC snap-in.

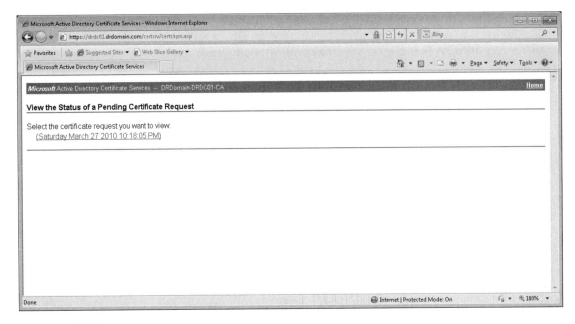

Figure 2.41 Certificate request status page.

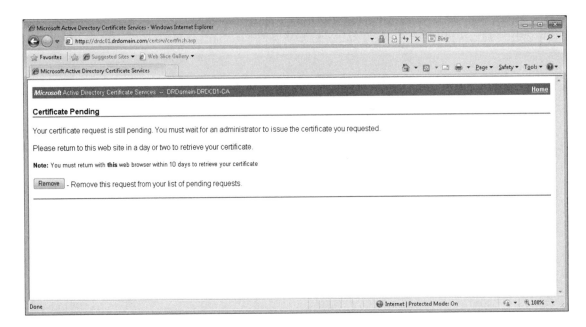

Figure 2.42 Certificate Pending page.

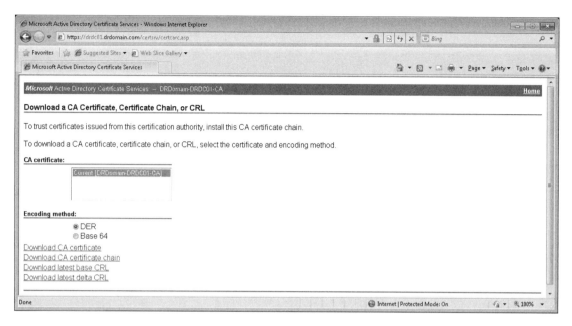

Figure 2.43 CA Certificate Download page.

Summary

Cryptography helps prevent unwanted system and data access. Cryptography solutions such as encryption and hashing are being used to hide data content. The data is scrambled in such a way that it can be unscrambled only by an authorized party. Each method for protecting data in this fashion has it advantages and disadvantages. As with anything, there are trade-offs. Some are faster than others. Some are more secure than others. You have to be informed so that you can use the best method or methods for your environment.

A Public Key Infrastructure provides a framework for securing your organization. Public or asymmetric key encryption algorithms are combined with digital certificates to provide authentication and encryption. It's important to understand that a true PKI system includes not only technology components but also policies. These policies govern the usage of keys and certificates within the organization. A key may be strong, but if its usage is not, then the ensuing security mechanism is not strong. Establishing a complete PKI solution requires a lot of planning and thought.

NETWORK SECURITY

INFORMATION IN THIS CHAPTER
- General Network Concepts and Vulnerabilities
- Network Services and Network Devices
- Internet Security and Vulnerabilities
- Network Security Tools and Devices

Network security is essential in today's world. Nowadays, a computer system is useless unless it is networked together with other systems. Networks are used to get information from point A to point B. That's what the world is all about—sending and receiving information. With the explosion of Internet, it's now easier and more convenient than ever. But along with the ease and convenience comes risk. It's almost riskier than ever to send information. The more methods that are developed to share information, the more exploits are developed.

General Network Concepts and Vulnerabilities

There are general network concepts that must be understood in order to get a better understanding of some of the more advanced concepts. The different network features and functions can take a variety of forms and can be implemented in a variety of ways. You have to understand these concepts and what they mean before you can understand the devices that implement them.

OSI Model

The OSI model is the Open Systems Interconnection model. It was developed by the International Standards Organization (ISO). The OSI model approaches network communication using

Security for Microsoft Windows System Administrators. DOI: 10.1016/B978-1-59749-594-3.00003-X a layered approach. Each layer consists of different protocols and functions. The OSI model has seven layers: physical, data link, network, transport, session, presentation, and application.

Physical Layer

The physical layer (Layer 1) is the lowest layer of the OSI model. The physical layer deals with device interaction with the physical medium. The physical layer references the bits and electric signals that travel through the network medium. Some examples of devices that exist at the physical layer are hubs, repeaters, and network adapters.

Data Link Layer

The data link layer (Layer 2) of the OSI model actually consists of two sublayers: the Media Access Control (MAC) sublayer and the Logical Link Control (LLC) sublayer. The MAC sublayer controls device interaction. The LLC sublayer deals with addressing and multiplexing. Physical addressing for network connections exists at the data link layer. The data link layer combines data bits into entities called frames. Network topologies like Ethernet exist at the data link layer. Network switches are the most common network devices that exist at the data link layer.

Network Layer

The network layer (Layer 3) of the OSI model controls logical addressing of network systems and devices. These logical addresses are used when one system wants to talk to another system. Network layer addresses are used not only to identify the system but also to determine what network the system resides on. The network layer combines multiple frames into units called packets. Routers are the most common devices that operate at the network layer. Some common protocols that exist at the network layer are Internet Protocol (IP), Internet Protocol Security (IPSec), and Internet Control Message Protocol (ICMP).

Transport Layer

The transport layer (Layer 4) of the OSI model controls link reliability. The transport layer is responsible for flow control and error control. The transport layer combines network packets into units called segments. The Transmission Control Protocol (TCP) and User Datagram Protocol (UDP) exist at the transport layer.

Session Layer

The session layer (Layer 5) of the OSI model controls connections between computers. These connections are called sessions. The session layer establishes, maintains, and terminates sessions between computers. The Network File System (NFS) and Server Message Block (SMB) protocols exist at the session layer.

Presentation Layer

The presentation layer (Layer 6) of the OSI model allows for interaction between different application layer implementations. The presentation layer provides somewhat of a translation between two different types of applications. Application layer implementations can use different formats and speak different "languages," as long as the presentation layer translates the data for them.

Application Layer

The application layer (Layer 7) is the highest layer of the OSI model. It's the layer that is closest to the end user. The application layer of the OSI model interacts directly with system applications. Some examples of application layer protocols include Hypertext Transfer Protocol (HTTP), File Transfer Protocol (FTP), and Simple Mail Transfer Protocol (SMTP).

Network Components

A network is divided into a variety of components. These components range from parts of a single computer to part of the network itself. Each of these components plays a different role in helping a network to function and pass information.

MAC Address

Every network device has a physical address called a MAC address associated with it. This MAC address is used to identify the device on the network. MAC addresses exist at the data link layer of the OSI model. MAC addresses consist of two parts. The first part identifies the manufacturer of the device. Each manufacturer has a different address assigned to it. The second part is assigned to the device by the manufacturer. MAC addresses are burned into the device by the manufacturer. In most cases, this address cannot be changed. Some devices, like network cards, however, have the capability to specify a new MAC address via software configuration. This new address is often called a Locally Administered Address (LAA). But even if you use an LAA, the original MAC is still present, so the configuration can be reverted at any time.

IP Address

An IP address is a logical address assigned to a network system. IP addresses exist at the network layer of the OSI model. IP addresses are defined by the IP in the TCP/IP suite. An IP is divided into two components: the network address and the host address. The network address represents the location of a group of computers. The host address represents the location of a single computer within a network. You can think of the network address as a street name and the host address as the house number. When you are looking at an IP address, the subnet mask is used to determine which portion of the address is the network address and which portion is the host address.

Originally, IP addresses consisted of only 32 bits. They were separated into four octets. But as the Internet grew, we began to run out these addresses. So a new version of IP addressing was developed. It is called IPv6. The original version then began to be termed as IPv4. IPv6 addresses contain 128 bits. This offers a greatly increased number of addresses. IPv6 addressing still has not taken off throughout the Internet. But usage is growing. IPv4 addresses still remain by far the most widely used type of IP on the Internet and inside companies.

There are five classes of IPv4 addresses: Class A, B, C, D, and E. The different classes are characterized by the number of networks available and the number of hosts available on each network. IP address class can be identified by their first octet. Table 3.1 outlines the characteristics of each class.

There are public IP addresses and private IP addresses. Public IP addresses can traverse the Internet. Private IP addresses cannot. Buying enough public IP addresses for everyone in your

Table 3.1 IP Address Classes

Class	First Octet Range	Number of Networks	Number of Hosts on Each Network
A	0 to 127	126 (0 and 127 are reserved)	16,777,214
B	128 to 191	16,384	65,532
C	192 to 223	2,097,152	254
D	224 to 247	Reserved for Multicast Addresses	Reserved for Multicast Addresses
E	248 to 255	Reserved for Experimental Use	Reserved for Experimental Use

organization can be a difficult task, not only because of the cost but also because of the limited availability of IPv4 addresses. What most organizations do is purchase a few public IP addresses for public-facing entities like external routers. They use private IP addresses for internal devices. Then, the company's router or firewall will do some sort of translation between the public and private IP addresses. There are certain ranges of IP addresses that have been designated as private by the Internet Assigned Numbers Authority (IANA). They are as follows:

Class A: 10.X.X.X
Class B: 172.16.X.X through 172.31.X.X
Class C: 192.168.X.X

Collision Domain

A collision domain is a network segment where network packets can potentially "collide." A network collision is when two systems attempt to send packets on the same physical segment at the same time. Both of the packets will be discarded. Both systems will then wait for a random wait period before resending their packets. Collisions happen only in networks where two different packets can be on the network at the same time. These are multiaccess network topologies like Ethernet.

Broadcast Domain

A broadcast domain is a network segment where network systems can reach one another through a message sent to the network's broadcast address. Devices on the same network subnet or VLAN are generally in the same broadcast domain.

NAT

NAT is Network Address Translation. NAT works at Layer 3 of the OSI model. NAT is used to hide the IP address of internal computers. NAT can be done for security purposes or for scalability purposes. You may not have enough public IP addresses available for all the systems on your network. As an example of how NAT works let's say Riley wants to connect to a Web server on the Internet. NAT would work as follows:

1. Riley's computer sends a request to the NAT routing using a private IP address.
2. The NAT router will map Riley's computer IP address to an outgoing network port. This mapping is stored in its mapping table.
3. The router will then contact the Internet Web server with a connection originating from the previously mapped network port and the router's externally facing public IP address.

4. The Internet Web server will then respond to the router's externally facing public IP address on the same port.
5. The router will then look that port up in its mapping table.
6. The router will then send the response back to Riley's computer.

PAT

PAT is Port Address Translation. It is very similar to NAT. Some people consider PAT a subset of NAT. PAT works at Layer 3 and Layer 4 of the OSI model. Not only does PAT hide the source IP address, it also hides the source port. This adds an additional layer of obfuscation.

DMZ

A DMZ is a network Demilitarized Zone. A DMZ is a network segment set aside to allow untrusted connections to a company's network resources. A DMZ usually sits between a company's internal network and the Internet. A company will put its externally facing Web servers in the DMZ, so if these servers are compromised, the company's internal network is still safe.

Network Services and Network Devices

Network communication consists of different services and devices. Each of these services and devices provides a different function. They also have their own vulnerabilities and exploits associated with them. You need to know what these vulnerabilities and exploits are in order to properly protect your organization.

DHCP

DHCP is the Dynamic Host Configuration Protocol. It is used to automatically provide IP addressing information to clients. A DHCP server can assign IP addresses, subnet masks, a DNS server address, and much more. This frees you from having to manually enter this information on all your client systems.

The problem with the DHCP process is that it uses broadcast messages. Clients do not know what DHCP server they should be contacting. They just accept information from the first one that responds. This can be trouble because someone could install a rogue DHCP server on the network. This could be done for malicious reasons or accidentally. Either way, it disrupts your network's operation. To combat rogue DHCP servers, Microsoft developed the concept of DHCP server activation. Unless a DHCP server is activated, it cannot service DHCP requests in your organization.

DNS

DNS is the Domain Name System. DNS is used to translate computer domain names to IP addresses. Computers are assigned domain names because domain names are easier to remember than IP addresses. In order for one system to talk to another system, they need to know each other's IP address. A DNS server is used to supply the systems with the IP addresses.

DNS servers contain special types of records. Here are a few:
- Address (A): It is used to map host names to IPv4 addresses.
- Address (AAAA): It is used to map host names to IPv6 addresses.
- Canonical Name (CNAME): It is used as an alias for another name.
- Name Server (NS): It is used to denote a DNS server.
- Mail Exchanger (MX): It is used to denote a mail server.
- Domain Name Pointer (PTR): It is used to point a domain name to an IP address.
- Start of Authority (SOA): It is used to denote the Start of Authority for a domain.
- Sender Policy Framework (SPF): It is used to validate e-mail sources. They help prevent e-mail spamming.
- Server selection or Service Location (SRV): It is used to denote a service residing on a server. Active Directory makes extensive use of SRV records to reference services.

DNS servers are often the victims of attempted denial-of-service attacks. The idea is that if someone can effectively deny access to a DNS server, then the clients who depend on this DNS server will not be able to get to any other servers or network services. You can protect against this through the use of a redundant DNS setup. You can use redundant hardware or set up secondary DNS servers.

Network Switches

In general, switches work at the data link layer (Layer 2) of the OSI model. Devices connected via a switch are on separate collision domain. Devices connected via a switch are in the same broadcast domain. Switches do filtering and forwarding based on MAC addresses. Switches keep a MAC table that lists all the devices that it has access to. When someone attempts to connect to a device, the switch knows which port to forward the request out on. If the switch does not know, then an ARP request will be sent. Based on who replies to the broadcast, the switch knows where to forward the traffic.

Routers

Routers work at the network layer (Layer 3) of the OSI model. Routers are used to connect two separate networks, often called subnets. These networks will be in separate broadcast domains. Routers use routing tables to keep track of routes between different networks. Sometimes, there are multiple paths to a given network. Routers will use routing metrics to determine the best, most efficient route to a destination.

Wireless Security and Vulnerabilities

Wireless networks offer a great degree of flexibility. Computers are not longer tied to a desk. They are free to move about your organization. Along with this flexibility, comes an increased administrative burden. The administrator must ensure that these wireless networks run efficiently and securely.

802.11 Standards

Most wireless networks adhere to one of the 802.11 technology standards. These standards define the equipment used to implement the network and the functionality supported. Each standard has different signal ranges, maximum bandwidths, and frequency ranges.

802.11a

802.11a networks operate at a frequency of 5 GHz. They support a maximum data rate of 54 Mbps. Because 802.11a networks use the less crowded 5GHz range, they do not really suffer much from interference. 802.11a networks do have a problem with range. 802.11a signals have a problem going through walls and other objects. This limited the standard's overall effectiveness and therefore hindered its widespread usage.

802.11b

802.11b networks operate at a frequency of 2.4 GHz. They support a maximum data rate of 11 Mbps. Because of the use of the 2.4GHz frequency range, 802.11b networks can suffer from interference. There are many devices like microwaves and cordless phones that also operate within this range. When the 802.11b networking standard was developed, the equipment used for the networks cost significantly less than 802.11a equipment. This lower cost helped increase uptake and acceptance of the standard. It was the first standard to gain widespread acceptance.

802.11g

802.11g networks operate at a frequency of 2.4 GHz. They have a maximum transfer rate of 54 Mbps. 802.11g equipment is compatible with 802.11b network equipment. This has aided in its uptake. 802.11g is currently the most rapidly growing standard for wireless connections, especially in home networks.

802.11n

802.11n is a relatively new wireless networking standard. 802.11n networks can operate at 2.4 or 5 GHz. 802.11n networks support throughputs from 54 Mbps up to 600 Mbps. 802.11n networks also offer compatibility with previous standards.

Wireless Encryption Protocols

Traditional networks use some sort of physical transmission media. You cannot gain access to these networks unless you can gain physical access to the transmission media. This makes it at least a little difficult to tap into these networks. Wireless networks do not have this limitation. Wireless transmissions travel through the air and can be accessed by anyone. This makes encryption increasingly important. There are currently two widely used standards for wireless encryption. They are WEP and WPA.

WEP Encryption

WEP is the Wired Equivalent Privacy protocol. Most wireless access points support the WEP standard. WEP is probably the most widely used wireless encryption standard. WEP, however, has known security vulnerabilities. There have been known cracks of WEP encryption. Because of these vulnerabilities, WEP is slowly being phased out in corporate networks.

WPA Encryption

WPA is the Wi-Fi Protected Access protocol. WPA was developed by the Wi-Fi allowance to be a secure wireless encryption protocol to replace WEP. WPA usage is growing in popularity. Originally, WPA only used a preshared key to establish encryption. But the standard has been expanded to include Extensible Authentication Protocol (EAP) extensions. WPA2 has begun replacing the original WPA standard. WPA2 increases security and adds more features from the new 802.11i network standard.

Wireless Vulnerabilities

Although wireless networks share some of the same vulnerabilities as wired networks, wireless networking does have a set of vulnerabilities that are specific to only that technology. A lot of them revolve around the widespread availability of wireless network access points. The easier something is to access, the harder it is to protect.

Lack of Authentication and Encryption

One of the most common vulnerabilities seen in wireless networks is the lack of authentication and/or encryption. It's possible that administrators may forget to enable authentication or encryption when they set up their wireless networks. Without encryption, anyone may connect to your wireless network. Without encryption, all your network traffic will flow in clear text. This makes it vulnerable to network sniffing. This can be avoided by ensuring that authentication and encryption are added to wireless networks.

Using Defaults

Using the default wireless network settings in your access point can introduce vulnerabilities into your network. If you use default settings, attackers don't have to try very hard to figure out how your wireless network is configured. One glaring mistake is the use of the default Service Set Identifier (SSID). Many vendors have a default SSID that is used in all their access points. Attackers may scan the airwaves using the default SSIDs from various vendors in an attempt to connect to an insecure network. So, even if you don't broadcast your SSID, using the default SSID puts you at risk because it is very easy for an attacker to guess what it is.

Eavesdropping

Wireless networks are very susceptible to eavesdropping. As long as someone is in a relatively close vicinity of the radio signals, they can pick up your wireless network. They don't have to be in the building. They could be in the parking lot. To protect against eavesdropping, you should secure your wireless network using authentication and encryption.

Rogue Access Points

In an attempt to access systems on your network, someone may set up a rogue access point. This is an unauthorized access point set up in your company's vicinity. Users in your company may then connect to this access point believing it to be an authorized one. The most effective way to combat this is through user education. Users should be educated as to which access points are safe to connect to. You can also periodically scan to see which access points show up within the vicinity of your company.

War Driving

War Driving is when attackers drive from location to location looking for a wireless network they can access. In general, they look for ones with no authentication. Once they find a network they can access, they attempt to sniff networks or try to connect to other systems on the network. There are two main ways to combat war driving. First, you can make sure your network is properly protected using authentication and encryption. Second, you can train your security staff to look for suspicious activity around the building and in the parking lot.

SSID Broadcasting

SSID broadcasting itself is not a vulnerability. But it does make it a little easier for an attacker to try to connect to your wireless network. In order for someone to connect to a wireless network, they need to know the network's SSID. If you are broadcasting your SSID, you have already given an attacker one piece of information he or she needs in order to hack into your network. So as a security precaution, you should disable broadcasting of your network's SSID, if possible. The problem is that if you are not broadcasting the SSID, anyone who wants to connect to the network will have to know it, in order to connect. In some instances, this may not be feasible.

Weak Encryption

Because wireless networks are more easily accessible by attackers, you need to ensure that you are using secure levels of encryption. Even though WEP is probably the most popular encryption method used in wireless networks, it's not the most secure. If possible, WEP encryption should be replaced with some form of WPA2 encryption.

Remote Access Technologies and Vulnerabilities

Remote access can mean a few different things. First, remote access to systems can simply be any access that doesn't occur from the system console. You could be on the corporate network, just not physical at the system console. Second, remote access could allow employees to access your corporate systems from noncorporate locations. Nowadays, the idea of a "mobile office" is putting more emphasis on the ability to provide this type of remote access. With remote access, it can be very difficult to determine who is actually accessing a system, especially when you start discussing access from remote locations. It's very important that appropriate consideration is taken when planning remote access to your systems.

Client Access VPNs (Virtual Private Network)

A virtual private network (VPN) establishes a private network connection through a public network, like the Internet. Some consider it a form of tunnelling. There are many types of VPNs. VPNs are often used to join two networks together. But what we want to looks at are client access VPNs. Client access VPNs are an extremely popular tool for providing external users access to a corporate network. The two most used technologies for this are IPSec VPNs and SSL VPNs.

IPSec VPNs use the IPSec protocol to create the VPN tunnel. IPSec VPNs operate at the network layer of the OSI model. When a client connects through an IPSec VPN, he or she has virtually full access to the network. Clients appear as just another node on the network. IPSec VPNs have been around for a long time. For years, IPSec VPNs were the standard for client access VPNs.

SSL VPNs have just begun to grow in popularity fairly recently. SSL VPNs use general SSL traffic over port 443 to establish the VPN connection. This is very useful when a user must initiate a connection from within a protected network. Many networks, especially corporate networks, filter what traffic is allowed to leave out through the firewall. In most cases, however, SSL over port 443 is allowed. SSL VPNs are considered most secure than IPSec VPNs because you have more control over what users can access. Another advantage SSL VPNs have over IPSec VPNs is the fact that most SSL VPNs can provide clientless access. Most IPSec VPNs require that some sort of VPN client software be installed on client systems in order for them to access the VPN.

Telnet

The Terminal Network or Telnet protocol is used to make virtual terminal connections to network devices. These devices could be computer systems or network equipment. Telnet can be used for remote shell connections or application connections. Telnet uses TCP port 23 for communications. By default, Telnet does not use authentication or secure connections. Although Telnet is still widely used, its lack of security has caused it to be replaced by Secure Shell (SSH).

Secure Shell (SSH)

SSH is being used as a secure replacement for Telnet. It uses public-key cryptography to verify the identity of the remote computer. SSH also provides for key re-exchange during the session. This helps to ensure continued security. SSH also supports secure tunnelling and X.11 connections. So not only authentication but also the sessions themselves can be secured. SSH uses TCP port 22 for making connections, although this port can be changed.

RDP

RDP is the Remote Desktop Protocol. RDP was developed by Microsoft as a protocol to be used for connecting to Windows desktops and servers running Remote Desktop Services (originally Terminal Services). RDP uses port 3389 by default. In order to make a connection, the client must be running a Remote Desktop Client. There are Remote Desktop Clients installed on all newer Microsoft operating systems.

Before you can use the Remote Desktop Client to access Windows 7 or Windows Server 2008 R2 systems, you must first enable Remote Desktop Services on the system.

Enabling Remote Desktop Services on Windows 7

1. From the Start menu, right-click **Computer** and select **Properties**. Or from the Control Panel, open the System applet.
2. In the left pane, select **Remote Settings**. This brings up the Remote tab of the System Properties window, as seen in Figure 3.1.

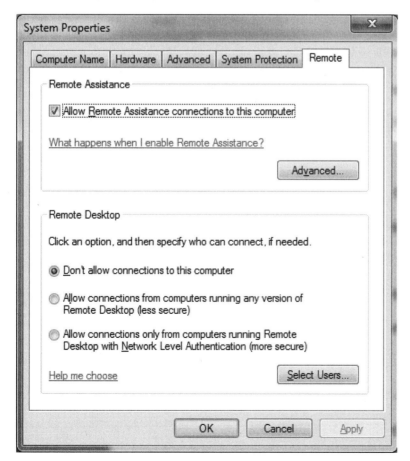

Figure 3.1 System Properties window – Remote tab.

3. In the Remote Desktop section, choose the option for Allow connection only from computers running Remote Desktop with Network Level Authentication.

Note: Users who are not running at least Windows 7 will not be able to make Remote Desktop connections to the system.

4. Click the button **Select Users**. This brings up the Remote Desktop Users window, as seen in Figure 3.2. Here, you can choose who will be able to access the system via Remote Desktop.

Figure 3.2 Remote Desktop Users window.

Tools & Traps

Remote Desktop Connection

The Remote Desktop Connection application is used to make connections to Remote Desktop Services. This application can be accessed from Start menu | Programs | Accessories. When you make a connection using this application, you are connected to a regular Remote Desktop session. The Remote Desktop Connection application also allows you to connect remotely to the console session of the server. In some cases, there may be actions you cannot perform in a regular Remote Desktop, and you will need to connect to the console session. Also, there is only a limited number of Remote Desktop connections allowed to a system. If this limit has been reached, you will not be allowed to make a new one until one of the others has been disconnected or unless you connect to the console session. To connect to a console session, run the command mstsc /admin. This will start the Remote Desktop Connection in console connection mode.

Note: There is a built-in group called Remote Desktop Users. The easiest way to give users Remote Desktop access to a system is to add them to this built-in group.

ICA

ICA is the Independent Computing Architecture protocol. It's a protocol developed by Citrix Systems used for remote connections to desktops and applications. ICA generally makes connections on TCP port 1494. But ICA can also be tunnelled inside the Common Gateway Protocol (CGP), also developed by Citrix, on port 2598. ICA has built-in compression that makes it highly useful over lower bandwidth connections.

IPSec

IPSec is Internet Protocol Security. IPSec operates at Layer 3 of the OSI model. It is used for securing communications between systems. IPSec authenticates and encrypts all the packets in a data stream.

IPSec starts by using an Internet Key Exchange (IKE) to negotiate which protocols and algorithms will be used in the communication. During the IKE, the keys that will be used for encryption are also exchanged between the two systems. The Authentication Header (AH) is used to authenticate and verify the packets that are being exchanged. Encapsulating Security Payload (ESP) is used to protect the data itself. ESP provides the encryption that is used to secure the data inside the packet.

Internet Security and Vulnerabilities

The Internet is an extremely useful tool. It puts an unlimited amount of information right at your fingertips and connects you to sources of information that you would never have been able to access just a few years back. The Internet and usage of the Internet are growing exponentially. But, unfortunately, so is the number of people trying to take advantage of others on the Internet. It's important that everyone understands not only the capabilities but also the dangers and how they can protect themselves.

General Internet Concepts and Vulnerabilities

The Internet is made up of a number of different components. It's a huge collection of different technologies that come together. Each of these components and technologies has its own role and function.

SSL and TLS

Secure Sockets Layer (SSL) is used to provide secure network communications. There were three versions of SSL. The fourth version was renamed to Transport Security (TLS). Although most people still refer to SSL usage, in many cases, what is actually being used is TLS. SSL and TLS work at the transport layer of the OSI model. They generally use a public-key algorithm for establishing encryption. SSL and TLS use x.509 certificates for handling key information.

HTTP and HTTPS

HTTP is the Hypertext Transfer Protocol. HTTP works at Layer 7 of the OSI model. HTTP generally uses port 80 for network communications. It is the main protocol used when accessing content over the Internet.

HTTP is based on a request-and-response system. For example, a user makes an HTTP request to a Web server. Then, the Web server sends back an HTTP response. HTTP uses a standard set of request types called verbs. When securing a Web server, it's important that you understand which verbs are required for your site. Some verbs are less secure than others. You want to make sure that you have disabled verbs that are not necessary for your site to function. Some of the most common verbs used are GET, POST, and PUT.

- GET: An HTTP GET is used for retrieving information from a Web server.
- POST: An HTTP POST is used to send information to a Web server, like when you fill in a form.
- PUT: An HTTP PUT is used to upload something to a Web server.

By default, information sent using HTTP is sent in clear text. This can present a problem when sending sensitive data or passwords. This is where HTTPS comes in. HTTPS is HTTP over SSL. With HTTPS, SSL or TLS is used to encrypt information sent using the HTTP. By default, HTTPS uses port 443 to send information.

Botnets

A botnet is a collection of agents called robots or bots that are used to perform automated tasks, usually malicious tasks. Botnets are used for spamming, distributed denial-of-service attacks, and many other exploits. In many cases, the bots that are performing these tasks are computers that have been compromised. So the owners of these computers may not be aware of what their computer is doing.

Because of their hidden nature, botnets are growing all over the Internet without widespread interference. Botnets can extend to hundreds of thousands, even millions of computers. Bots can be programmed with methods used to infect other computers and create other bots.

The computers in a botnet are controlled by a central server called a command-and-control server. The command-and-control server sends out periodic instructions to the computers in its botnet. In some cases, there can be more than one command-and-control server in a botnet. This makes it even more difficult to stop. You may find and shut down one command-and-control server, but the bots will then just receive instructions from another command-and-control server in the botnet.

Botnets themselves can be hard to detect and take down. But there are a few things you can do to protect your organization. First, make sure antivirus software is installed and up-to-date on all your systems. This will help prevent systems from being infected. You can also purchase heuristic-based intrusion detection systems. These systems can help identify infected systems. Network monitoring can also be used. You should look for excessive network traffic between systems or excessive traffic destined for a single external system.

Peer-to-Peer File Sharing

Peer-to-Peer File Sharing systems are no longer just a new fad technology. They have become ingrained in our Internet culture. You have to remember that just because Samantha is hosting a file that she says is a video of the Olympics, that doesn't mean that it really is the Olympics. It could be some sort of Trojan or malware. Nowadays, many botnets are built using Peer-to-Peer File Sharing systems.

Most corporate organizations do not use Peer-to-Peer File Sharing systems for business purposes. So the easiest way to protect against abuse is to take steps to prevent their usage within your organization. You can do this by blocking access to any external servers or services that are used to control the peer-to-peer software. You can also internally block any ports that are used by peer-to-peer systems to talk to each other.

Denial-of-Service (DOS) Attacks

Denial-of-service (DOS) attacks attempt to prevent normal usage of a system or service. DOS attacks can take many forms. An attacker may send a malformed or bad request to a system, hoping that request will cause the system to crash. An attack may also send a flood of valid requests to a system, hoping that the system cannot handle the volume of requests being sent. This volume may either cause the system to crash or just prevent the system from processing valid requests.

Oftentimes, in order to implement a successful denial-of-service attack, you need to have more than one performing the attack. This is especially the case when the attack is attempting to flood the device with requests. This is called a distributed denial-of-service attack (DDOS). The perpetrator of a DOS attack will recruit other systems to help perform the attack. Oftentimes, these other systems will be part of a botnet. The DOS coordinator will install software or agents on the infected system that will cause them to send the desired requests to the system under attack.

Malware

Malware is a general name given to software developed for malicious purposes. Most computers that access the Internet have some sort of malware installed on them, usually without the owners' knowledge. The only thing they may notice is that their computer is a little slower or less responsive than before. But they don't know what to attribute it to. Two common types of malware most people encounter are spyware and adware.

Spyware

Spyware is a type of malware used to spy on user activity on a computer. Spyware will gather information on users' habits such as browsed Web sites, accessed applications, and downloaded programs. This information is then sent to an attacker, so he or she knows what attacks can be perpetrated on a system. Spyware can have even more direct effects, like stealing of passwords and credit card information. This type of information can lead to direct financial benefits for an attacker. Spyware is generally not self-proliferating. It is not spread from infected system to infected system. Usually, spyware is downloaded from a Web site or server that the user believes contains beneficial software. In fact, many times, spyware will be bundled in a download with some sort of legitimate software.

Adware

Adware is a type of malware that is used to display advertisements on infected systems. Adware may display a series of pop-up ads on infected systems in an attempt to direct traffic to those sites. These pop-up ads can be annoying, and the sites that are being advertised can also be malicious. Some adware programs can replace ads that show up on legitimate Web sites. In these cases, the user would assume that the products and services being advertised are legitimate because they show up on a legitimate site.

Browser Security

Most of the content on the Internet is accessed via a Web browser, like Internet Explorer or Firefox. Your Web browser is the main interface between your computer and the Internet. It's important that you understand what capabilities exist in your browsers. It's also important that you understand the vulnerabilities introduced in a browser.

General Browser Security Concepts

Each Web browser is different and has different features. But there are certain concepts and technologies that are implemented in all browsers. They may be implemented differently in different browsers, but the core functionality is still there.

JavaScript

JavaScript is a scripting language understood by most browsers. Many Web sites use JavaScript to perform tasks that cannot be performed with simple HTML code. Scripts written using JavaScript are processed on the client side. This is what causes the potential for damage to be done to a client system. Malicious Web sites can insert JavaScript into their Web pages. These scripts can be used to perform actions on the client system. JavaScript can be used for files access, file upload, cache access, and changing certain system settings. You can use your browser's security settings to govern how JavaScript will be run on your system.

Java Applets

Java is a platform used for creating operating system independent applications. These applications are called Java applets. All you need to have installed on the system is a Java Virtual Machine (JVM). The Java applets will run inside this Java Virtual Machine. Java applets are much more robust than scripts written in JavaScript. Therefore, they can also be much more dangerous. One thing you can do to protect against systems running malicious Java applets is to require your system to run signed only Java applets. A digital signature will help to ensure that the application is created by a known entity that can be tracked.

ActiveX Controls

ActiveX is a technology Microsoft developed to allow robust applications to be run inside of a Web browser. The applications written for this technology are called ActiveX controls. ActiveX controls can be embedded inside the Web browser itself. They can then be activated by various Web sites. ActiveX controls have the capability to perform a lot of system-level functions. Because of this, they can be very dangerous. But you can configure whether or not to allow your system to execute ActiveX controls.

ActiveX Settings in Microsoft Office: In addition to being able to use ActiveX controls in Internet Explorer, you can also use ActiveX controls in Microsoft Office documents. Because of this, Microsoft Office allows you to configure when and how ActiveX controls can be used. As seen in Figure 3.3, these settings are configured under Trust Center | ActiveX Settings. You have the following options:

- Disable all controls without notification
- Prompt me before enabling Unsafe for Initialization (UFI) controls with additional restrictions and Safe for Initialization (SFI) controls with minimal restrictions
- Prompt me before enabling all controls with minimal restrictions
- Enable all controls without restrictions and without prompting (not recommended; potentially dangerous controls can run)

You also have the option to enable Safe mode for ActiveX controls. Safe mode will apply a set of predetermined restrictions to limit the access of ActiveX controls.

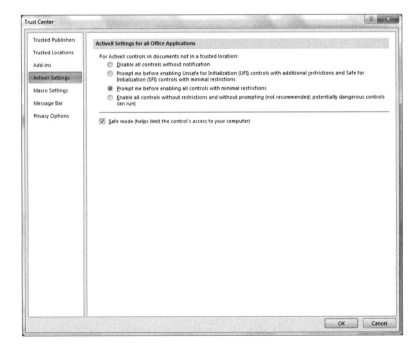

Figure 3.3 Microsoft Office ActiveX Settings.

XSS (Cross-Site Scripting)

Cross-site scripting is when an attacker attempts to use someone else's Web site to execute his or her code. Different Web sites can have different abilities to execute scripts on your system. There are also Web sites where you would be more apt to allow a script to perform actions on your system. In a cross-site scripting attack, an attacker attempts to fool you and your system into thinking that a trusted site is the one actually executing the script. This is often done by using a specially formed URL sent in an e-mail link.

For example, you may want to go to http://arlenes-trusted-site.com/page.aspx. But instead, you may be sent to http://arlenes-trusted-site.com/page.aspx? http://claudes-site/execute-claudes-script.aspx. In this example, you are going to arlenes-trusted-site, but you are executing a script from claudes-site. The problem is that there is something wrong with the page.aspx file on arlenes-trusted-site that allows you to execute arbitrary code. This vulnerability needs to be fixed on arlenes-trusted-site. In fact, most cross-site scripting vulnerabilities are a result of a flaw on a trusted site.

Cookies

Cookies are small files that are stored on computer systems to store user information. This information could be preferences, site settings, personal information, or browsing habits. In general, the use of cookies is a very effective way of storing information that can be used by Web sites. Without cookies, you might have to reenter personalization information every time you visited a Web site.

Many feel that cookies that store user information are an invasion of privacy. Cookies may contain a lot of personal information. This information could then potentially become available to sites that you did not intend to be able to view this data.

Securing Internet Explorer

Internet Explorer is the Web browser most commonly used on Windows systems. If you are using Internet Explorer, it's important that you understand some of the security measures in place to protect your system. The most prevalent of which is the configuring of security zones.

Security Zones

In order to help simplify protecting Internet Explorer, Microsoft developed the concept of security zones. Instead of attempting to apply a one-size-fits-all approach to security settings, you can have different settings for different security zones. A security zone represents the level of trust you have in a Web site. You set specific browser settings for each security zone. Then, depending on which zone a particular Web site falls into, it will have those settings applied. Internet zones are configured on the Security tab of Internet Options. Each zone has default settings that are already configured, but they can be customized to fit your needs. There are four security zones in Internet Explorer: Internet, Local intranet, Trusted sites, and Restricted sites.

Internet: Internet sites are basically sites that do not fit into any other zone. Most of the sites you encounter will fall into the Internet zone. By default, Internet zone settings are set to Medium-high, as seen in Figure 3.4.

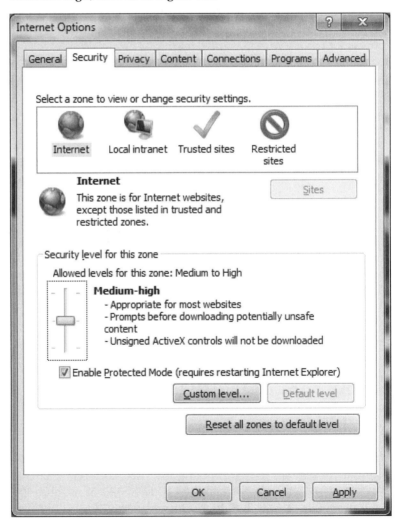

Figure 3.4 Internet Explorer Internet zone.

Local intranet: The local intranet zone is intended for sites that exist on your local LAN. The theory here is that you would have a greater level of trust for sites that exist on your local network. By default, the Local intranet zone has settings set to Medium-low, as seen in Figure 3.5.

To determine which sites will be categorized as part of the intranet zone, click the **Sites** button. This brings up the Local intranet window, as seen in Figure 3.6.

If you want, you can have Internet Explorer automatically determine which sites should be a part of the Local intranet zone, based on the requirements you specify. You can also manually specify which sites to add to the Local intranet zone. This is done by clicking the **Advanced** button in the Local intranet window. This brings up the Local intranet Add Sites window, as seen in Figure 3.7.

Trusted sites: Trusted sites are sites that you explicitly trust. You know these sites to be safe. Trusted sites have an even more relaxed level of security. Some features and functions require that sites be in the Trusted sites zone in order for them to work properly. By default, the Trusted sites zone has its settings set to Medium, as seen in Figure 3.8.

You can manually specify which sites you want to be added to this zone. You can do this by clicking the **Sites** button. This brings up the Add Trusted Sites window, as seen in Figure 3.9. By default, you can only add HTTPS sites as trusted sites, but this can be changed by unchecking the option for Require server verification (https:) for all sites in this window.

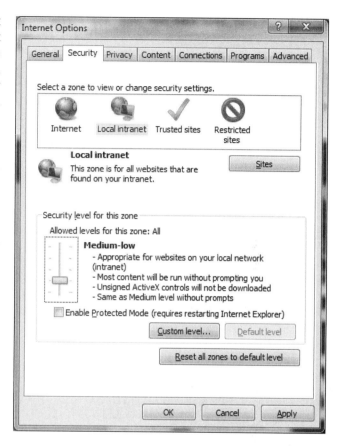

Figure 3.5 Internet Explorer Local intranet zone.

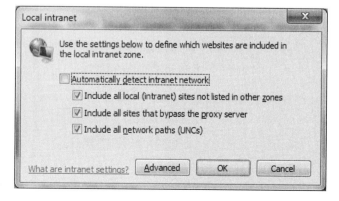

Figure 3.6 Internet Explorer Local intranet window.

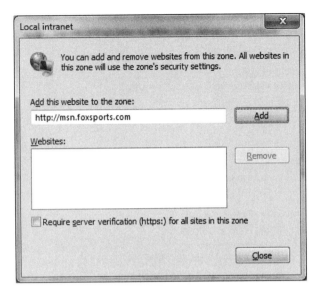

Figure 3.7 Internet Explorer Local intranet Add Sites window.

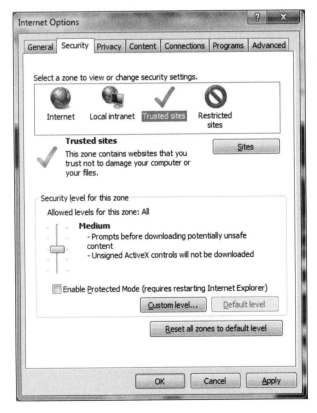

Figure 3.8 Internet Explorer Trusted sites zone.

Restricted sites: The Restricted sites zone is for sites known to be potentially harmful to your system. This is the most restrictive security zone available. By default, settings for the Restricted zone are set to High, as seen in Figure 3.10.

You have to manually add sites to the Restricted zone. This is done by clicking the **Sites** button. This brings up the Add Restricted sites window, as seen in Figure 3.11.

E-mail and Messaging Security

E-mail and messaging systems provide an easy method for users to communicate with one another. E-mail and instant messaging systems provide similar functionality, but they serve different purposes. They are also implemented very differently. These differences mean they have different vulnerabilities and are secured differently.

E-mail Concepts and Vulnerabilities

E-mail is short for electronic mail. E-mail messages are sent from a client to an originating e-mail server, to a destination e-mail server, and to the receiving client. Each of these entities can save a copy of the message. E-mail is used for personal use and business use. This is one difference between e-mail and instant messaging systems. Instant messaging is generally used for personal use.

E-mail Spam

Spam is bulk e-mail sent out to individuals who neither requested nor expected to receive a message. Spamming is usually done for two reasons. First, spam may contain some sort of advertisement. Someone may send out spam in an attempt to get people to buy something. The second reason is to cause e-mail disruption. The large volume of e-mails being sent out can cause problems for e-mail messages. E-mail systems may be so busy processing spam e-mails that they cannot process legitimate e-mails.

Spam may be sent out to random e-mail addresses or to the e-mail addresses of people who used their e-mail address to sign up for something. Some companies sell valid e-mail addresses to spammers. So you may use your e-mail address to sign up for something you want, but end up getting spam, which you don't want. The privacy policy of a Web site will generally give you an idea of whether they might sell your e-mail address to someone else.

There are a couple of things that can be done to protect against spam. First, you can educate users about where to and where not to enter their addresses. Have them check a Web site's privacy policy before they register their e-mail addresses on the site. You can also install spam filters on your e-mail servers. Spam filters are specific applications designed to detect spam. Spam often has certain keywords in the subject or body of the message. For example, if your company sells paper products and there is an e-mail coming in that offers "Male Enhancement," it's probably spam, and the spam filter will detect it and prevent it from being delivered.

E-mail Hoaxes

E-mail hoaxes are e-mails circulated that spread some sort of false information. But the intent of the e-mail is not to spread misinformation; the intent is to affect the functioning of e-mail

Figure 3.9 Internet Explorer Add Trusted Sites window.

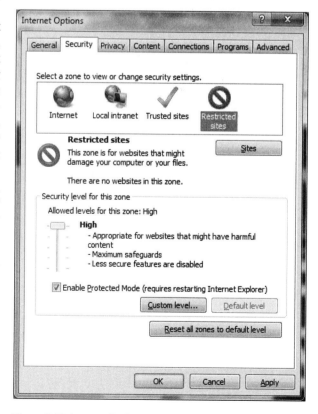

Figure 3.10 Internet Explorer Restricted sites zone.

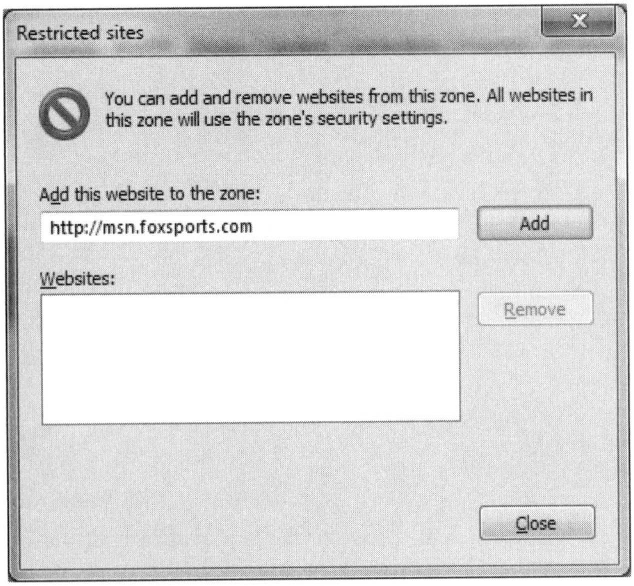

Figure 3.11 Internet Explorer Add Restricted sites window.

systems. Generally, e-mail hoaxes will include something to the nature of "forward this to everyone you know, so they are aware, too." So Shawn will forward to Leo and Isaac. Leo will forward to Victor and Pam. Isaac will forward to Jayden, Shyheim, and Denzil, and so on, and so on. Before you know it, everyone in your organization will be forwarding the e-mail around. The volume of hoax e-mails being forwarded may affect your system's capability to process legitimate e-mails.

To help prevent e-mail hoax problems, you can educate your user population not to forward nonbusiness e-mails. Many times e-mail hoaxes may contain false information about some new computer virus that is going around. Users may think they are doing something good by forwarding these e-mails around. There are Web sites that keep track of legitimate and fake viruses. Users can use one of these sites to verify the information in the e-mail, instead of assuming it to be true.

SMTP Relay

SMTP relays are basically servers that are used to forward SMTP messages. SMTP relays can help you protect your internal e-mail servers. An SMTP relay server can be used to forward messages that are destined for or originating from the Internet. This way your internal e-mail servers are not exposed directly to the Internet. The problem occurs when there are what's called "open" SMTP relay servers. Open SMTP relay servers are those that are not secure; they allow anyone to send a message through them. Spammers use open STMP relay servers to forward e-mails through. If your SMTP relay service is open, your system may be spamming without your knowledge. Eventually, your server may end up on an e-mail blacklist. This could greatly hinder your company's capability to send legitimate e-mails.

If you are not using SMTP relay, you should make sure that your e-mail servers have the service turned off. If you are using the service, you should make sure the service is secure. You should limit who can send e-mails through your SMTP relay server. If your SMTP relay is only for internal forwarding, you should also limit where your SMTP relay server can send e-mails.

Instant Messaging

Instant messaging (IM) systems can be very useful. It allows immediate and convenient communication between two parties. If you use an externally administered system, then you don't have to worry about managing the infrastructure. But along with the convenience and ease of IM come many potential threats. With IM, you have to worry about information flowing in clear text, Internet links in messages, file transfers, and social engineering.

Information sent via IM is generally sent in clear text. There are programs available that can be used to encrypt IM traffic, but these are usually separate add-ons. If someone is sending sensitive information via IM, that information is vulnerable to network sniffing.

You have to be very careful with IM systems because you never really know who is on the other end. IM systems allow you to post Internet links inside of messages. This can be very dangerous. The links you receive could direct you to malicious sites. Many e-mail systems can scan messages for dangerous links, but IM generally does not do this. IM clients may warn you about clicking links in messages, but they will not block them.

IM clients also allow file transfers. Usually, these are just pictures or something harmless. But that's not always the case. Sometimes, these files are malicious executables. IM clients do not scan messages to see if these files are malicious or not, by default. It's up to the users to use their best judgment.

Social engineering attacks are also common with instant messaging systems. Because of their relaxed and informal nature, IM systems often give people a false sense of familiarity and trust. You must still remember that you do not really know who is on the other side of the connection. If you send confidential information through an instant message, you need to be aware that you could be sending it to anyone.

There are several steps that can be taken to secure instant messenger usage. First, you can prevent the usage of external IM clients. Most public e-mail clients require users to log into a central authentication system. You can block users within your network from accessing this central authentication server. If you need IM within your organization, you can set up an internal IM system.

If preventing the use of external IM systems is not feasible, then you should do what you can to protect the users and client systems. You can use an add-on application to encrypt the content of your IM messages. This will help protect against network sneaking. IM encryption applications generally require the use of a shared key. The key is usually exchanged the first time communication occurs. Second, you should enable the file transfer protection settings in the IM client. Certain antivirus applications also have plug-ins for IM clients. You can use these to scan transferred files for malicious content. Finally, end-user education is essential. You can educate users not to click links in e-mail messages. You can also educate users on the dangers of instant messaging in an attempt to help prevent social engineering attacks.

Network Security Tools and Devices

In addition to general network security devices, there are tools and devices developed specifically for network security. Depending on the organization, these devices may be administered by the company's security team or by the company's networking team. It depends on whether you consider network security a subset of networking or a subset of security.

Proxy Servers

A proxy server is an intermediate server that sits between a client and resources the client is trying to access. A proxy server will make requests on behalf of the client. The client never talks directly to the resource. Proxy servers can serve many functions. They mask the IP of the client making the request. Proxy servers can speed up Web page access through the use of caching. Pages can be pulled from the cache on the proxy server instead of downloading the page from the Internet. Proxy servers can also be used to scan and monitor traffic to and from the Internet.

Clients can be configured to use proxy servers in a few different ways. The proxy server can be manually specified. You can have your browser automatically detect the proxy server. Or you can use a proxy configuration file. We'll walk through configuring a proxy server in Internet Explorer and Firefox.

Configuring a Proxy Server in Internet Explorer

1. Inside Internet Explorer, go to Tools | Internet Options.
2. Go to the Connections tab, as seen in Figure 3.12.
3. In the Local Area Network (LAN) settings, click **LAN settings**.
4. In the LAN Settings window, as seen in Figure 3.13, you can configure your system's Proxy Server settings. If you need to

configure a SOCKS Proxy or you want to configure Proxy exceptions, click the **Advanced** button.
5. In the Proxy Settings window, as seen in Figure 3.14, you can configure a SOCKS Proxy, by unchecking the box for Use the same proxy server for all protocols and entering the name of the SOCKS Proxy Server.

Configuring a Proxy Server in Firefox

1. Inside Firefox, go to Tools | Options.
2. Under the Advanced menu, as seen in Figure 3.15, go to the Network tab.
3. In the Connections section, click **Settings**.
4. On the Connection Settings window, you can configure your system's proxy settings. Figure 3.16 shows Firefox configured to use a Proxy Server called drproxy01. drdomain.com.

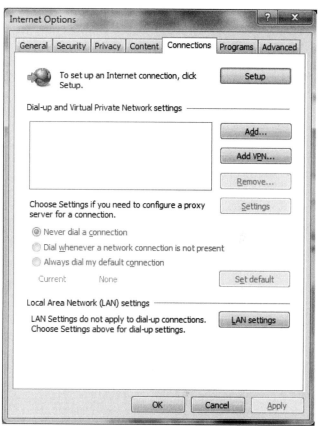

Figure 3.12 Internet Explorer Connections tab.

Network Firewalls

Firewalls are used to separate two networks. Most often they are used to separate an internal corporate network from an external public network. Firewalls can also be used to create a DMZ. Firewalls can also be used to separate internal networks. You may have certain areas of your network that you want to secure the general network traffic. You may want to separate your user network from your infrastructure network or your data network.

Firewalls can be implemented using hardware or software. Many software firewalls come preinstalled on hardware with a hardened OS. There are three general types of firewalls: packet filtering, stateful inspection, and application gateway.

Packet-Filtering Firewalls

Packet-filtering firewalls operate at the network layer (Layer 3) of the OSI model. Packet-filtering firewalls make processing decisions based on network addresses, ports, or protocols.

Packet-filtering firewalls are very fast because there is not much logic going behind the decisions they make. They do not do any internal inspection of the traffic. They also do not store

Figure 3.13 Internet Explorer
LAN Settings window.

Figure 3.14 Internet Explorer
Proxy Settings window.

any state information. You have to manually open ports for all traffic that will flow through the firewall.

Packet-filtering firewalls are considered not to be very secure. This is because they will forward any traffic that is flowing on an approved port. So there could be malicious traffic being sent, but as long as it's on an acceptable port, it will not be blocked.

Stateful Inspection Firewalls

Stateful inspection firewalls keep track of connection status. Ports can be dynamically opened and closed if necessary for completing a transaction. For example, when you make a connection to a server using HTTP, the server will initiate a new connection back to your system on a random port. A stateful inspection firewall will automatically open a port for this return connection.

Stateful inspection firewalls are considered more secure than packet filtering firewalls. Stateful inspection firewalls process application layer data. Therefore, they are able to take a deeper look into the transaction to understand what is going on.

Application Gateway Firewalls

Application gateway firewalls operate at the application layer (Layer 7) of the OSI model. They filter access based on application definitions. Application definitions can include not only port numbers but also specific application information like acceptable HTTP verbs. Application gateway firewalls are considered to be some of the most secure firewalls available because of their capability to inspect packets and ensure the packets are conforming to application specifications.

Because of the amount of information being processed, application gateway firewalls can be a little slower than other firewalls. Sometimes, people use application gateway firewalls in conjunction with another firewall. The application gateway firewall will be used only to protect servers. Or the application gateway firewall will sit behind the other firewall. The first firewall will be used as a first-level filter. The application gateway firewall will process only packets that pass through the first firewall.

Personal Firewalls

Personal firewalls are system-level firewalls that are used to protect a system from network-based threats. Personal firewalls control what ports your system is allowed to listen on. They also control what processes on your system are allowed to make network connections. Many antivirus vendors include personal firewalls.

Windows Firewall

The Windows Firewall is used to protect your Windows system from network-based threats. You can control who has access to your system and what access is granted. The Windows Firewall applet allows you to configure these firewall settings. In the Windows Firewall section of the Control Panel, you have two options: Check firewall status and Allow a program through Windows Firewall.

Check firewall status: This option brings up the Windows Firewall window, as seen in Figure 3.17. This

Figure 3.15 Firefox Advanced Network section.

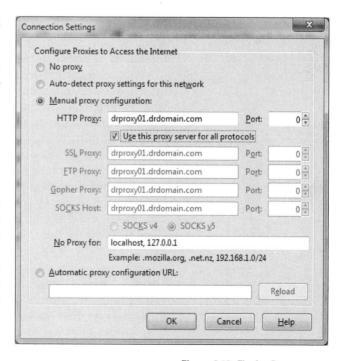

Figure 3.16 Firefox Proxy Settings.

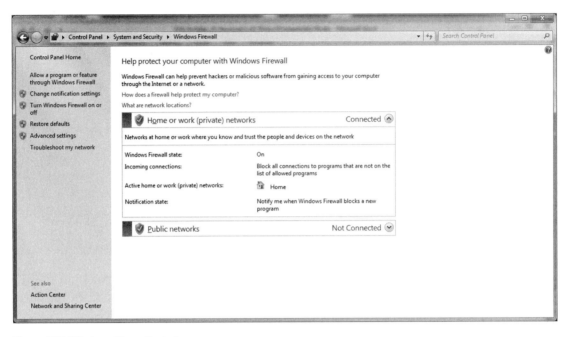

Figure 3.17 Windows Firewall window.

option will allow you to see if Windows Firewall is enabled or disabled on your system. You can also see Windows Firewall settings for incoming connections and notifications.

Allow a program through Windows Firewall: This option brings up the Allowed Programs window, as seen in Figure 3.18. Here, you can see what programs are allowed by Windows Firewall. If you want to change these settings, you must choose the **Change settings** option. You can now select a program to allow access to and what networks the program is allowed to communicate on. The **Details** option will show you the path to the executable for the application being allowed. If you want to allow a program not listed, you can choose the **Allow another program** option. You can then specify the location of another program you want to allow through the firewall.

Honey Pots

Honey pots are systems set up to attract hackers. They are set up in such a way that hackers will have access to them. Monitoring honey pots allows you discover ways in which a hacker may attack your systems. You can use the data discovered to secure your important systems.

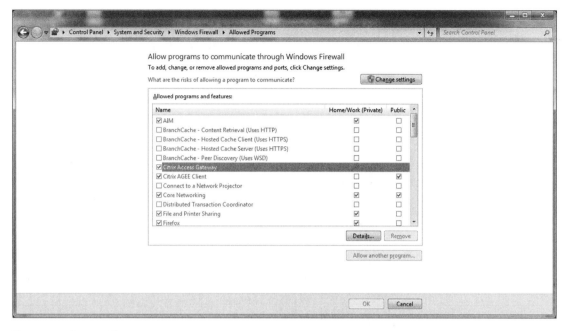

Figure 3.18 Allowed Programs window.

Network Tools

Ipconfig: The *ipconfig* command is used to manage the IP config-uration of your system. You can use it to view IP information on your system, like your IP address, subnet mask, and DNS server. Or you can use it to manage IP configuration information. You can clear your DNS cache or renew your DHCP settings. Ipconfig usage is shown in Figure 3.19.

Ping: The ping utility is used to test connectivity between two systems. Ping sends Internet Control Message Protocol (ICMP) echo request messages to the target system and waits for an ICMP reply. If a reply is received, then you know there is basic network connectivity between the client system and the target system. Ping usage is shown in Figure 3.20

Tracert: Tracert is the Windows implementation of the tracer-oute utility. Tracert is used to check connectivity between two sys-tems at a more granular level. Tracert will actually show you the path between two systems. If there is a failure in connectivity, tracert can also help you pinpoint where in the route the failure occurred. Tracert usage is shown in Figure 3.21

Nslookup: Nslookup is used for querying a DNS server. You can use it to test name resolution on your system. Nslookup can tell you

Figure 3.19 IPconfig usage.

Figure 3.20 Ping usage.

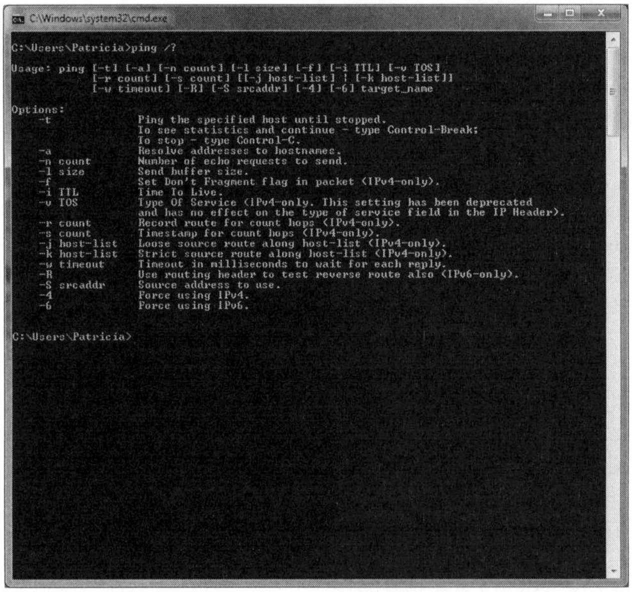

what DNS server your system is using to look up domain names. It can also tell you what the response is. If you are having trouble connecting to a system, it could be because the name is not resolving or resolving to the wrong address. Windows uses SRV records in DNS for pointing clients to services. You can use nslookup to determine what server is assigned to carry out a particular service. Nslookup usage is shown in Figure 3.22.

Netstat: Netstat is used to show network statistics and connections. You can use it to determine what systems a client is connected to and vice versa. You can also use it to determine what ports a system is listening on. This can be very useful if you think a system may be propagating a virus. Or if you think the system may be connected to a botnet. Netstat usage is shown in Figure 3.23.

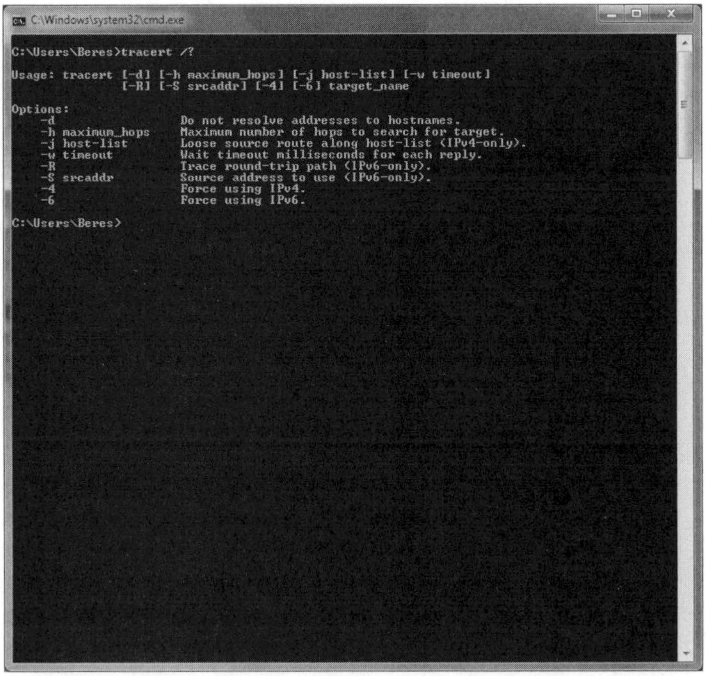

Figure 3.21 Tracert usage.

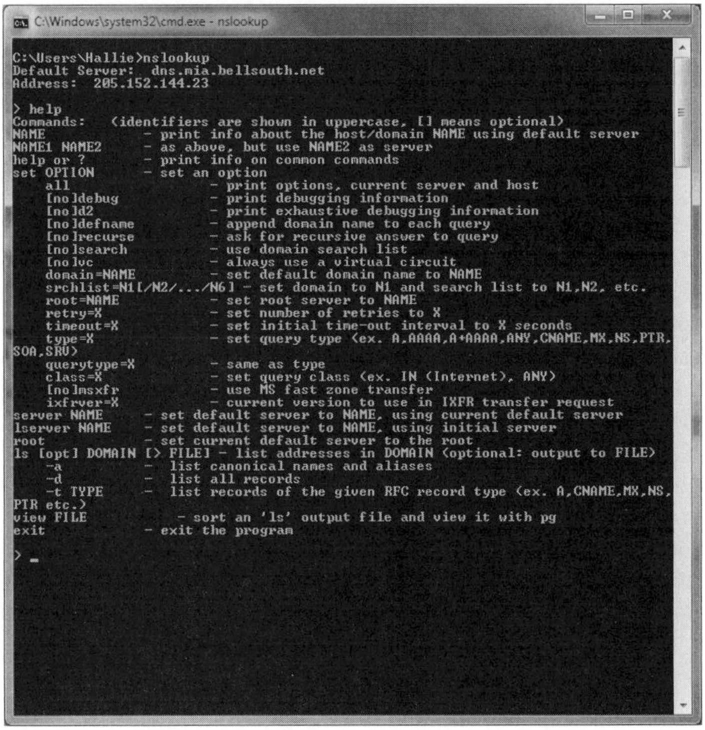

Figure 3.22 Nslookup usage.

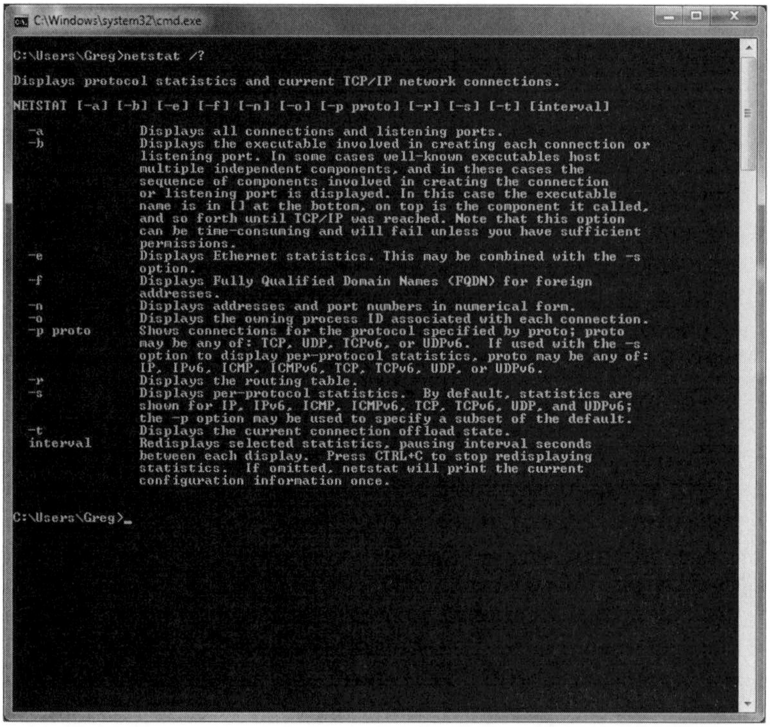

Figure 3.23 Netstat usage.

Summary

A good understanding of networking and networking components will help give you a better understanding of some of the vulnerabilities that affect these components. Considering the fact that nowadays almost all computers are connected to some type of network, it's increasingly important that you understand how to protect against network threats. Most attacks are actually initiated via a network, and most viruses are spread through a network. So in many instances, a good network security plan will help protect against the proliferation of attacks and system compromises.

The Internet, which is actually the largest network in the world, is also the most dangerous. You can have no idea of the true intentions of the people and systems you come across on the Internet. Because of this, you should treat all Internet traffic as hostile. In some cases, it may be unwarranted, but it's better to be safe than sorry. The most common interface to the Internet is the Web browser. It's key that you understand what mechanisms are in place to secure the Web browsers used on your systems. For your physical networks, firewalls and proxies provide your basic protection. Your firewall is often seen as the fence separating you from the outside world. This fence needs to be secured and consistently monitored.

SYSTEM SECURITY

INFORMATION IN THIS CHAPTER

- General System Security Threats
- Hardware and Peripheral Devices
- OS and Application Security
- Virtualization
- System-Based Security Applications

System security is crucial in any environment. After all, the systems are the main components of the environment. The network is important, but your company's assets do not physically reside on the network. All your files and data reside on some system. There are many different types of system vulnerabilities and threats. There are general threats that apply to all systems. There are vulnerabilities and threats that apply to hardware and peripheral devices. The operating system and the applications that exist on top of the operating system have their own vulnerabilities. There are also specific vulnerabilities that are introduced when you choose to use system virtualization. You also need to be aware of the different applications available to protect your systems against threats.

General System Security Threats

Certain threats and vulnerabilities are inherent to all systems. These threats are not specific to any particular type of system, like file servers and print servers. They are everywhere. They are threats to servers, client systems, just about any system in your environment. You need to look out for privilege escalation, viruses, worms, Trojans, and rootkits.

Security for Microsoft Windows System Administrators. DOI: 10.1016/B978-1-59749-594-3.00004-1

Privilege Escalation

Privilege escalation is using a vulnerability to gain privileges other than what was originally intended for the user. There are two main types of privilege escalation: horizontal and vertical. You need to understand these types of privilege escalation and how to protect against privilege escalation in general.

Horizontal Privilege Escalation

Horizontal privilege escalation is when a user gains the access rights of another user who has the same access level as he or she does. That might sound a little weird. You might wonder why someone would want to gain the rights of someone at the same level as that person. Here's an example. Let's say Robin and Liz both have accounts with the same financial institution. They have the same account types and account profiles. Robin may attempt to gain access to what Liz has access to, meaning Liz's account. So, although they both have the same access levels, Robin can benefit from having access to Liz's account. Robin can then transfer or withdraw money out of Liz's account.

Vertical Privilege Escalation

Generally, when someone attempts to hack into a system, it's because they want to perform some action on the system. This could be damaging the system or stealing information. Oftentimes, this requires a privilege level the attacker does not possess. This is where vertical privilege escalation comes in. Vertical privilege escalation is when an attacker uses a flaw in the system to gain access above what was intended for him or her. This is what most people think of when they hear privilege escalation.

Protecting Against Privilege Escalation

There are many vulnerabilities that can lead to privilege escalation. Some of the most common are cross-site scripting, improper cookie handling, and weak passwords. Cross-site scripting and improper cookie handling can be protected against programmatically. Weak passwords require end-user education and the setting of password requirements. You can set requirements for password complexity and password age limits. There are two other widely used methods of preventing privilege escalation. They are the principle of least privilege and the separation of privileges.

When you are dealing with software, the principle of least privilege suggests that software modules or processes only have rights to perform the actions intended to be done by that module or process. The module should not have access to any other parts

Tools & Traps

Service Accounts

You have to be very careful with service accounts. Remember, when you specify a particular account for a service, everything that service does runs in the context of that user. If that service were to be compromised, the attacker would basically have the rights of the account that was used to run the service. You also need to be especially careful with services that can be used to run other commands, for example, the scheduler service. Let's say Ileana wants to execute a command that requires administrative privileges that she doesn't have. If your scheduler service runs with a service account that has administrative privileges, Ileana can schedule the command prompt to run. When the scheduler starts the command prompt, it will be running with administrative privileges. Then, every command Ileana executes in the command prompt will run with administrative privileges.

of the application, operating system, or file system. This way, if there is a vulnerability in that process and it is compromised, the attacker will only have access to a very limited area of the system.

Separation of privileges goes hand in hand with the principle of least privilege. Separation of privileges is dividing a program or process into smaller parts. Each of these parts has specific duties to perform.

Viruses

Viruses are unwanted code that runs on systems, generally without the owner knowing it. The term virus is often misused to classify all types of malicious software. But, in actuality, viruses do have specific characteristics. First, and most importantly, viruses attempt to spread from one computer to another. But they do not move by themselves. Some type of human action is required. An infected file must be accessed somehow by the target computer. This could be via e-mail, transferred via removable media, or being on a shared network location. Also, viruses generally must be activated by a user action. This is why many viruses try to attach themselves to legitimate files. When a user accesses the legitimate file, the virus will be activated.

Boot Sector Viruses

There is a class of viruses called *boot sector viruses*. The boot sector is the first sector on a hard drive. Information in a system's boot sector is loaded into memory when the system first boots up. So, placing a virus in the boot sector can ensure that the virus will always be activated right away.

Macro Viruses

There is also a class of viruses called *macro viruses*. Macros are little mini programs that run inside document processing programs, like Microsoft Word and Excel. Generally, you use macros to automate the execution of a repeated task. Over the years, macros have become increasingly more powerful. They can now reach outside of the confines of the program in which they are executed. With this power, comes danger. Macros can be extremely useful when used for legitimate purposes. But they can be just as dangerous when used for malicious purposes. This was the reason for the development of the macro virus.

Macro viruses are basically macros written to execute malicious code. They take advantage of the hooks macros can have into your system. An attacker may just take a *vbscript* that he or she has written and wrap it in a macro. Macro viruses can read information of your system and send it to an attacker. They can also change your system's configuration settings.

Macro Security

You can use general methods like antivirus and user education to protect your system against macro viruses. But you can also take it one step further and configure macro security settings inside Microsoft Office applications. This is done through the Trust Center, as shown in Figure 4.1.

Your options for Macro Settings are as follows:

- **Disable all macros without notification** Selecting this option will disable all macros. Users will not be notified that macros are disabled.
- **Disable all macros with notification** Selecting this option will disable macros. Users will receive a notification message letting them know that macros are disabled.
- **Disable all macros except digitally signed macros** Selecting this option will allow digitally signed macros to execute, if you trust the publisher. If you do not trust the publisher, you will be notified and given a chance to manually execute the macro. If a macro is not signed, it will be disabled without notification.
- **Enable all macros (not recommended; potentially dangerous code can run)** This option will allow all macros to execute. Choosing this option will leave your system completely open to macro viruses.

You can also optionally configure Developer Macro Settings. You can set the option for Trust access to the VBA project object model. This option enables or disables the Visual Basic for

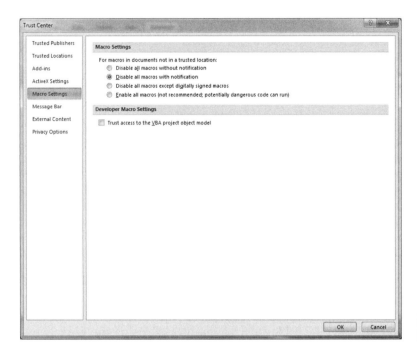

Figure 4.1 Microsoft Office Macro Settings.

Applications environment. With this option enabled, Visual Basic can be used to automate Office programs.

Polymorphic Viruses

In most cases, viruses are identified by their footprints. Their footprints consist of their file names, files they infect, and registry keys they infect. Most virus-scanning software looks for these pieces of the footprint when they scan systems. In order to help avoid detection, coders have written viruses to be polymorphic. Polymorphic viruses attempt to change their footprints, in order to help prevent detection. Polymorphic viruses can change their file names, and in some cases, they can add blank lines to their code in order to change the file size. This makes the virus even more difficult to detect.

Worms

Worms are sometimes considered to be a form of a virus. But there is one key characteristic of worms that separates them from viruses. Worms are self-replicating. They transfer themselves from one system to another. They do not require any human interaction to copy or e-mail them to another system. They also do not have to attach themselves to other files in order to be activated. They are self-activated.

The damage caused by worms can be two fold. First, they cause damage to the systems that are infected with them. Second, because they copy themselves from system to system, they can cause network issues. A worm propagating from system to system can easily eat up your network's bandwidth.

Protecting Against Worms

Because worms propagate themselves through the network, there are a few network precautions that you can take to prevent their propagation. You can use access control lists on your routers to prevent traffic from being propagated on certain ports or to and from certain machines. You can also use firewalls or network packet filters to filter packets that carry suspicious payloads.

Trojans

Trojans are also sometimes referred to as Trojan horses. This comes from the story of the Trojan horse in Greek mythology. The Greeks gave the Trojans the Trojan horse as a gift. The Trojans allowed the gift inside their kingdom. But inside the horse were Greek soldiers who attacked the Trojans. Computer Trojans are similar. They will either disguise themselves as useful applications or attach themselves to a useful application. This way, users will activate the Trojan without knowing they are doing any harm. Trojans, like viruses, are not self-replicating. They require user interaction to move from one system to another. Trojans are mostly used to allow attackers to gain remote access to a system. The attacker may try to copy information from the system or gain keyboard control of the system.

Logic Bomb

Logic bombs are viruses or Trojans that are activated after a certain event happens or a certain time period passes. Logic bombs can be separate files or inserted in other pieces of code. People often use logic bombs as jokes. For example, someone may create a logic bomb that activates on April 1, that says April Fools.

Rootkits

A rootkit is a malicious program designed to take full control of a system. The name comes from the "root" account on a UNIX system. The root account has full control over the system. Rootkits are generally not self-propagating. Human interaction is required to move them from system to system. In fact, rootkits are often targeted at specific systems.

Rootkits can take many forms. They can originate from viruses or Trojans. Rootkits are usually built using defects in drivers or other kernel-level programs. That's because kernel-level programs operate at the lowest system level, therefore having the deepest level of access to the system. Rootkits try to hide their presence on the target system. Some rootkits will delete or disable the system security logs. Rootkits can also modify operating system tools that would be used to detect them, like process lists.

Hardware and Peripheral Devices

Hardware and peripheral security take different forms. First, you have to worry about securing access to the devices and protecting them from theft. This mostly comes in the form of physical security. Then, you have to worry about security vulnerabilities built into the devices themselves. Many hardware devices come with software built into them called firmware. Firmware controls how the devices will behave in certain circumstances. Like with any software, firmware can present vulnerabilities that you need to be aware of.

Hardware Security

At the physical level, hardware security means protecting devices from tampering or theft. Although theft of the device itself is bad, in many cases, it's the theft of the data that may be on the device that causes the real problem. So you also need to protect against this.

Computer Systems

Usually, you will not find people trying to physically steal servers or desktops for that matter. What you will find is people trying to steal laptops. Laptops are easy to carry and easy to hide. The question is "what can be done about this?" First, you should never leave your laptop in an insecure area, like a conference room. You should also be careful about leaving your laptop in your car. You may come back to find not only your window broken but also your laptop missing. If you have to leave your laptop somewhere, try to make sure it is out of plain view. This way, you are not presenting a tempting situation.

Hard Drives

If your system is stolen, there are measures you can take to protect the data on your hard drives from being accessed. In Windows, you could use the Encrypting File System (EFS) to encrypt the files on the disk. Without the right key, the data cannot be uncrypted. You can also use BitLocker to encrypt the drive.

BitLocker encrypts the entire drive, not just individual files. This way, when new files are added to the drive, they are automatically encrypted. Using BitLocker is considered much more secure than just using EFS.

Removable Media

Removable media, like CDs, DVDs, and flash drives, can represent another security risk. They are easy transportable. This makes them easily stolen. In order to protect these devices, you should use some type of encryption to encrypt sensitive files. USB flash drives support many of the same protection methods as regular hard drives, like EFS and BitLocker. Many USB flash drives also come with software that you can use a password to access them.

Peripheral Device Security

Peripherals present some of the same potential issues as removable media. Peripheral devices can be easily stolen. But some devices present additional concerns because of the technologies they use.

Bluetooth

Bluetooth uses radio waves to transmit data. Bluetooth is becoming ever more popular for communicating between devices. There are a large number of Bluetooth devices available today. There are Bluetooth-enabled computers, mice, keyboards, phones, and headsets. Bluetooth can provide a quick and easy method for sending short communications or transferring small amounts of data.

Bluejacking

Bluejacking is the practice of sending unsolicited messages to someone's Bluetooth connection on his or her phone, computer, and so on. Bluejacking is often used to send advertising messages out to people's phones.

Bluesnarfing

Bluesnarfing is hacking into someone's phone via the Bluetooth connection. You can use this connection to send e-mails and text messages or to view contacts and calendar information. Most of these require that the attacking device and hacked device be "paired." One way to combat Bluesnarfing is not to leave your device in "discoverable" mode. If your device is not in discoverable mode, it's harder for the attacking device to find it.

OS and Application Security

Securing your operating system and applications is core to securing your system. Although there are viruses and malware written for hardware and peripheral devices, what you mostly have to worry about securing are the operating systems and the applications. OS hardening and application patching are key to making sure that your systems are secure.

OS Hardening

Operating systems have default settings that take not only security into concern but also usability. In many cases, usability will win out over security. So, when you first install an operating system, it is not as secure as it could be. OS hardening is the process of further securing an operating system to eliminate potential vulnerabilities.

General OS Hardening Techniques

Every operating system has different measures that can be taken to make them more secure. But there are some general techniques that can be used on almost all operating systems. The steps to implement these techniques may be different for each operating system, but the concepts are still the same.

Decreasing the Attack Surface

The attack surface of your operating systems represents all the possible attack entry points. The more services and applications you have running on your system, the more entry points and the greater the attack surface. To decrease the attack surface of your system, you should disable all unused services. The Services applet shown in Figure 4.2 will list the services that are installed on your system. It will also tell you whether the services are running or not and whether they are set to start automatically. The Services applet can be accessed from the Start menu | Programs | Administrative Tools.

You should also uninstall any applications or components installed on your system that are not being used or that are not necessary. This includes removing unused Roles from your Windows 2008 R2 systems. Applications and components can be uninstalled from Windows 7 systems using the Program and Features applet in the Control Panel, as shown in Figure 4.3.

Selecting the option for Turn Windows features on or off will open the Windows Features window, as shown in Figure 4.4. Simply deselect all the features or components that are not needed on the system.

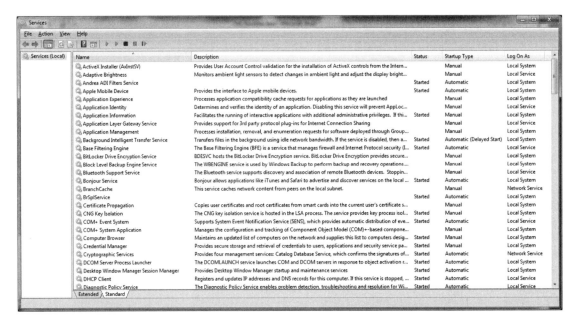

Figure 4.2 Services Applet.

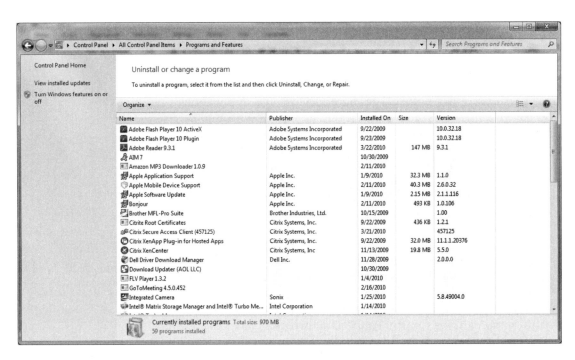

Figure 4.3 Programs and Features applet.

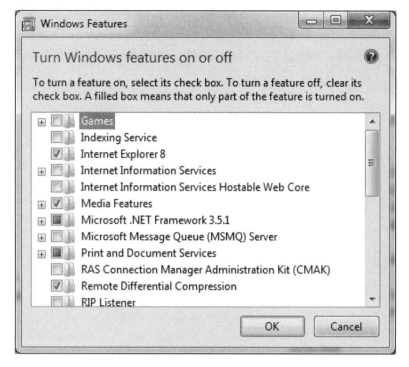

Figure 4.4 Windows Features window.

On Windows Server 2008 R2 systems, you use Server Manager, as shown in Figure 4.5, to remove roles that do not need to be on your server. Server Manager is accessed from the Start menu | Programs | Administrative Tools.

Account Security

You can also harden your operating system by taking certain precautions with regard to user accounts. You can start with ensuring that you use strict password rules. You should set rules for complexity and age.

You should also disable or remove unused accounts. The more user accounts you have, the greater the chance an attacker may be able to guess or brute force a password. Many systems include a guest account. Unless you plan to use this account for a specific purpose, which could not be accomplished by another account, you should be sure to disable all guest accounts.

Another popular security technique is to disable or rename the default administrator account. In order for an attacker to gain access to an account, he or she needs to know the account name and the password. If you have changed the name of the administrator account, he or she will need to find out both the name and the password used by the administrator. By default, Windows 7 systems have the default administrator account disabled.

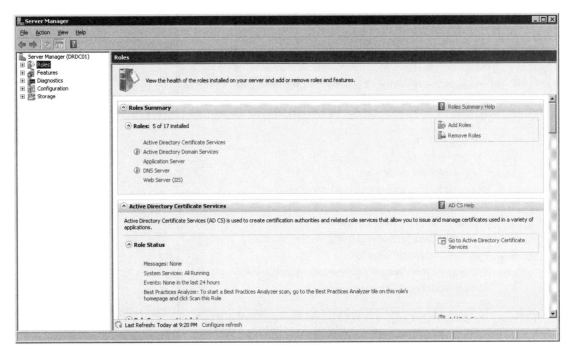

Figure 4.5 Server Manager.

On Windows 7 systems, these changes can be made in the Local Users and Groups snap-in, as shown in Figure 4.6. You can access this snap-in through the Computer Management applet. The Computer Management applet is accessed from the Start menu | Programs | Administrative Tools.

To make these changes for domain users, use the Active Directory Users and Computer applet on your Active Directory domain controller, as shown in Figure 4.7. The applet is accessed from the Start menu | Programs | Administrative Tools.

Windows OS Hardening

Windows operating systems provide specific tools that can be used for OS hardening. They allow you to systematically tighten security for the entire operating system. They help you by suggesting settings that will help you achieve your desired security level.

Security Configuration Wizard

In order to help in the process of hardening Windows operating systems, Microsoft developed the Security Configuration Wizard (SCW). The SCW uses a roles-based approach to securing the system. Based on the roles performed by the system, the

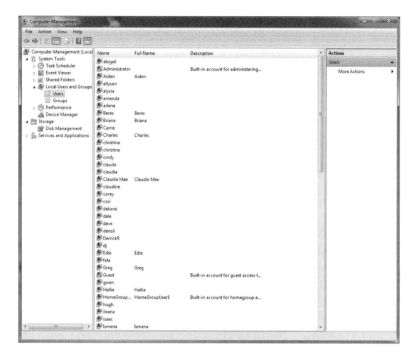

Figure 4.6 Local Users and Groups snap-in.

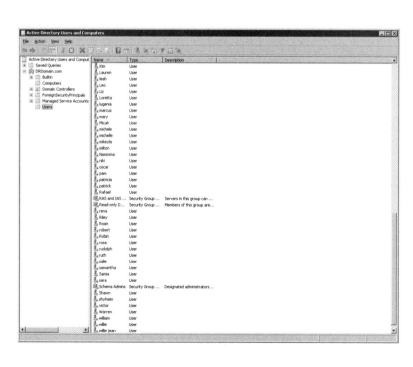

Figure 4.7 Active Directory Domain Users and Computers applet.

SCW will suggest the security settings that should be deployed. After you have deployed the desired roles to your system using the Add Roles wizard in Server Manager, you run the Security Configuration Wizard and select the roles you want on your system. The Server Configuration Wizard will not only secure the system for the roles you want but also disable the services, ports, and so on for the roles you do not want.

User Account Control

Many viruses and different types of malware attempt to make system-level changes to your operating system. You can help prevent this by using User Account Control. User Account Control is used to control when programs can make changes to your system. User Account Control Settings are available through the User Accounts applet in the Control Panel. Inside the applet, just select the option for Change User Account Control Settings. This will bring up the User Account Control Settings window, as shown in Figure 4.8.

User Account Control Settings has four options:

- Always notify: The user will always be notified when either the user or a program attempts to make changes to the system.
- Notify me only when programs attempt to make changes to my desktop: The desktop will be dimmed when these attempts are made. This is the default option.

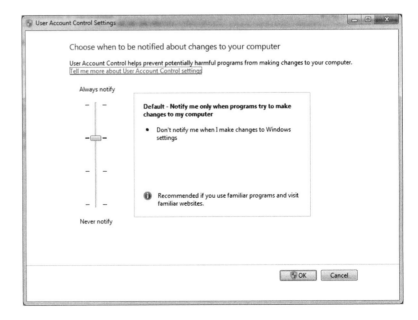

Figure 4.8 User Account Control Settings window.

- Notify me only when programs attempt to make changes to my desktop (do not dim my desktop): The desktop will not be dimmed when these attempts are made.
- Never notify: The user is never been notified when either the user or programs attempt to make changes to the system.

Patching and Updating

Patching and updating are a crucial part of a security strategy. Vendors constantly put out patches for security vulnerabilities. These patches do not do any good unless you apply them to your systems. In fact, when a vendor puts out a patch for a vulnerability, it alerts attackers to the vulnerability. So if you do not implement the patch, you are leaving yourself open to an attack.

Hotfixes

Hotfixes are generally small fixes for one or maybe two issues. It depends on the vendor, but usually, hotfix testing by the vendor is not very extensive. Hotfix testing is usually very targeted. Vendors test the new code, and they test for regressions in modules affected by the code change. Depending on the issue, a vendor may deliver a public hotfix or a private hotfix. Public hotfixes are posted and available to everyone. Private hotfixes have to be requested from the vendor. Private hotfixes may be done for specific issues that only a handful of customers may be experiencing. The vendor may not want to put out a public hotfix, which would be consumed by everyone.

Service Packs

Service packs are generally a collection of hotfixes. Sometimes, service packs also include new features. Service packs are almost always released publicly. It's very seldom that you will see a private service pack, unless the service introduces new features that would have to be licensed. Because of the size the of service packs and the amount of changes being made, service packs usually go through a rigorous testing process.

Patch Management

Patch management is not just about installing patches. It's having a comprehensive system for identifying, testing, deploying, and tracking patches.

The first thing you need to do is identify all the items that will need to be patched. Your environment will consist of different operating systems, applications, tools, and utilities. Each of these components could be patched using a different method. So, your patch management plan must account for these.

Next, you must determine how you will check for updates. Some vendors send electronic bulletins. Some vendors require you to visit their Web sites to find updates. Some applications have a built-in mechanism for checking for updates. No matter what the method, you need to make sure that you check for updates on a regular basis. The more often you check, the better.

Before you deploy updates and patches to your production environment, you should deploy them to a test environment. Vendors test patches and updates before they deploy them, but their test environment probably does not completely match your production environment. You should test these patches in an environment that mirrors your production environment. First, you should test to ensure that the patch or update fixes the issue it was defined for. Next, you need to ensure that the patch or update does not cause problems with other parts of your environment. Having a repeatable set of regression tests will make the effort more systematic and easier.

Next, you need to have some method of deploying the patches and updates. You can use each vendor's default method. Or you could use a third-party application or tool to install all patches and updates.

After the patches have been installed, you need some way of tracking them. You need to keep track of which patches were installed to which systems and when they were installed. This will help to ensure that you do not unknowingly have unpatched servers. Usually, whatever method you used to apply the patches will have some way of tracking which patches have been installed. If not, you may need to invest in a third-party tool.

Windows Update

Windows Update is the system developed by Microsoft for updating Windows systems. Windows Update can be used to download patches, hotfixes, and service packs. You can update your Windows operating system and other Microsoft software. Windows Update can be accessed from the Control Panel or on the Start menu | Programs.

Installing Updates

The first thing you will see when you open Windows Update is the summary shown in Figure 4.9. Windows Update will show you what updates are available for your system. Windows

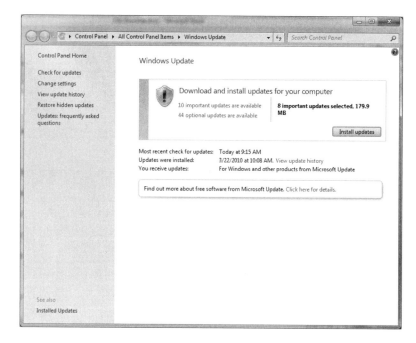

Figure 4.9 Windows Update.

Update will tell you how many important updates and how many optional updates are available. It will also show you the total file size for all the updates that have been selected.

If you click either hyperlink telling you how many important and optional updates there are, you will be taken to the Select updates to install screen, as shown in Figure 4.10. Here, you can choose which option and which important updates to install. Once you have selected your updates, click **OK** to return to the Windows Update summary screen. If you click the **Install updates** button, your updates will be installed.

Change Settings

Windows Update allows you to configure how the update process will be handled on your system. To configure your Windows Update settings, inside Windows Update, select **Change settings**. This will bring up the Change settings window, as shown in Figure 4.11.

You can configure the following settings in Windows Update:

Important updates: This section allows you to configure how important updates will be handled. You have four options:

- Install updates automatically (recommended) – specify date and time
- Download updates but let me choose whether to install them

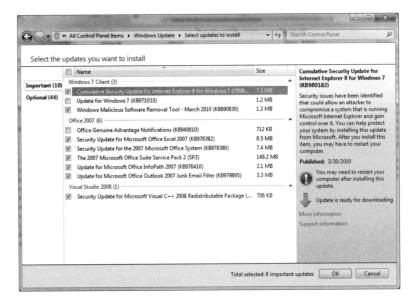

Figure 4.10 Windows Update – Select updates to install screen.

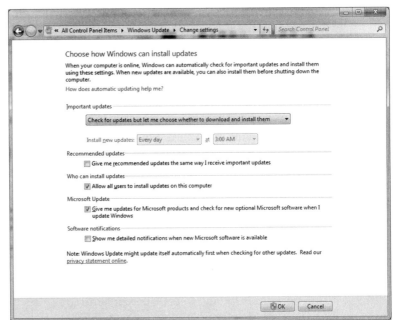

Figure 4.11 Windows Update – Change settings window.

- Check for updates, but let me choose whether to download and install them
- Never check for updates (not recommended)
  Recommend updates: This section allows you to configure how recommended updates will be handled. You have one option:
- Give me recommended updates the same way I receive important updates

Who can install updates: This option allows you to configure who can install updates on the system. You have one option:

- All users to install updates on this computer

Microsoft Update: This option allows Windows Update to check for updates for other Microsoft products, not just the operating system. You have one option:

- Give me updates for Microsoft products and check for new optional Microsoft software when I update Windows

Software notifications: This setting determines whether you will receive notification messages for new Microsoft software. You have one option:

- Show me detailed notifications when new Microsoft software is available

Installed Updates

To see what updates have been installed on your system, click **Installed Updates** in the lower left corner of the Windows Update window. This will bring up the Installed Updates window, as shown in Figure 4.12. You can see which Microsoft updates have been installed. You can also see updates from vendors that have chosen to integrate with Windows Update standards.

If needed, you can also uninstall updates from here. Just right-click an update and choose **Uninstall**.

Figure 4.12 Windows Update – Installed Updates window.

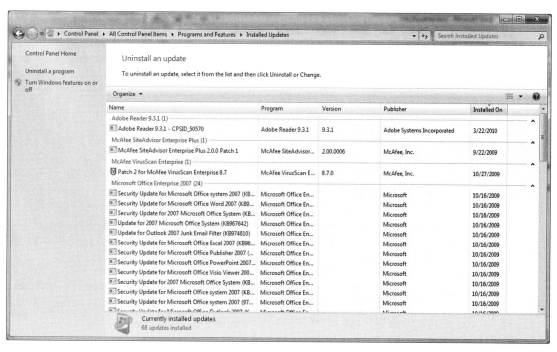

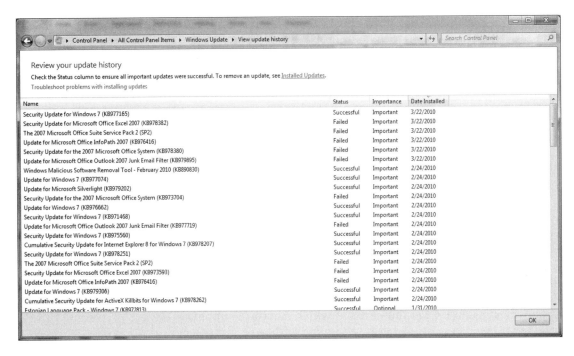

Figure 4.13 Windows Update – View Update History window.

View Update History

This will bring up the View Update History window, as shown in Figure 4.13. Here, you can view a log that shows what updates were installed and when they were installed. You can also see when updates attempted to install, but the updates failed.

If you right-click an update and click **View details**, it brings up the Details window, as shown in Figure 4.14. Here, you can view detailed information for the update, like when it was installed and the update type. If the installation failed, you can see the error code here.

Restore Hidden Updates

Every time you run Windows Update, it will check for available updates. There will be some updates that you do not want to install. By default, this update will show up every time you run Windows Update. In order to keep the update from showing up every time, you can hide the update. To hide an update, simply right-click the update in the update list and select **Hide update**. Now, you will no longer be prompted to install the update.

There may be a time when you want to restore the update so that it can be installed. On the Windows Update summary screen, select the option for **Restore hidden updates**. This brings up the Restore hidden updates window, as shown in Figure 4.15. Here,

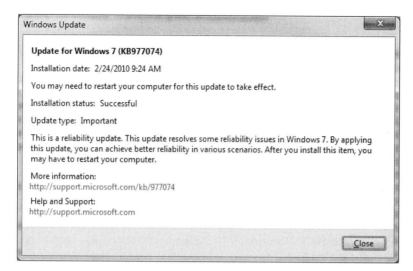

Figure 4.14 Windows Update – Update Details window.

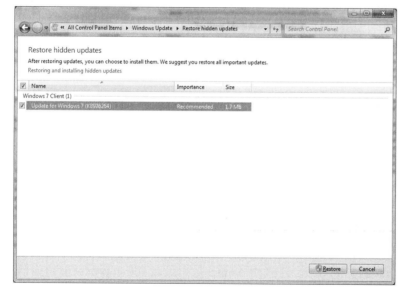

Figure 4.15 Window Update – Hidden Updates window.

you can restore updates that you have hidden from the system. Simply select the box next to the update and click **Restore**. The update will not show up in the available update list.

Virtualization

There are many types of virtualization. But what we are concerned with here is hardware or system virtualization. With hardware virtualization, an abstraction layer is used to hide the physical hardware in the system. Virtual systems called virtual machines are then installed on top of this abstraction layer. Virtualization allows you to install multiple virtual systems on top of one physical system. This help increases the density of your data center and can save you a lot of money in space, power, and cooling. You can virtualize server and client operating systems.

Hypervisors

Hypervisors are used to provide an abstraction layer to separate the virtual machines from the system hardware. This allows you to install a virtual machine with any operating system without having to worry about getting the right device drivers for the hardware platform. The hypervisor also separates virtual machines from each other. So, if one virtual machine is having issues, it does not affect the operation of the other virtual machines. There are two types of hypervisors: Type 1 and Type 2.

Type 1 Hypervisors

Type 1 hypervisors are hardware-level or bare-metal hypervisors. Type 1 hypervisors are installed directly on top of the hardware platform. Because Type 1 hypervisors sit directly on the hardware, there is usually less overhead than with Type 2 hypervisors. This can increase capacity and overall performance of the system.

Type 2 Hypervisors

Type 2 hypervisors are software-level hypervisors. Type 2 hypervisors are installed on top of an existing operating system. Because Type 2 hypervisors can install on top of an existing operating system, they are more convenient than Type 1 hypervisors. For example, when you want to test a hypervisor, you don't have to dedicate a specific machine for it. You can use an existing machine with an existing operating system.

Hyper-V

Microsoft's hypervisor is called Hyper-V. It is a Type 1 hypervisor that is commonly mistaken for a Type 2 hypervisor. This is because there is a client-servicing operating system running on a host. But that operating system is actually virtualized and is running on top of the hypervisor. Hyper-V is installed on Windows Server 2008 R2 systems using the Add Roles wizard in Server Manager.

Virtualization Security

The widespread acceptance of system virtualization is growing rapidly. But it's still a relatively new technology that presents new security concerns. These new security concerns require new methods of protection.

Antivirus software is used to protect systems from viruses, malware, and so on. Normally, you might install antivirus software on all your physical systems. With virtual systems, this changes a bit. You want to minimize the amount of RAM and processing power used by each virtual machine. So installing the antivirus software on each virtual machine is probably not the most efficient usage of resources. You may want to consider using an in-line network-based solution. The in-line device can scan traffic destined for and leaving the physical servers. This ensures that your systems are protected, but decreases the amount of resources used by each virtual machine.

You also have to worry about hypervisor-level rootkits. Hypervisor-level rootkits take advantage of the virtualization capabilities of a processor. These rootkits can intercept commands sent by the operating system. This allows them to take full control over the system.

System-Based Security Applications

There are security applications aimed specifically at performing system security functions. Some of these applications are free. Some must be purchased. Either way, you should perform a thorough evaluation of any product before you deploy it in your environment. Not all these programs provide the same level of protection or support. Many times, you will have to deploy a combination of them to adequately protect your environment.

Antivirus Software

Antivirus software is the most common system security product. Nowadays, antivirus is used as a general term for a collection of different products. Antivirus packages may include antivirus capabilities, antispyware capabilities, personal firewall capabilities, and much more. Antivirus packages may include different modules for scanning e-mail, Web servers, and other components. A thorough testing process will help determine which modules are needed in your environment.

You also have to worry about compatibility. Some antivirus vendors have limited operating system support. Some may support client operating systems and not server operating systems. If you are using Remote Desktop Services, you have to make sure the antivirus product you purchase supports this type of environment, as many do not.

The effectiveness of an antivirus is determined by the detection method used. There are two main methods in use today. Most use a signature-based approach. Some use a heuristic-based approach. In a signature-based approach, the antivirus software keeps a catalog of different virus signatures. When files are scanned, the antivirus software looks for a pattern that matches one of the signatures in the catalog. In the heuristic-based approach, a pseudo-signature is created. This pseudo-signature is a more loosely matching signature. They look for more general characteristics. There doesn't have to be an exact match. This allows the heuristic-based approach to catch a wider variety of viruses, including those that are polymorphic.

Microsoft Security Essentials

Microsoft Security Essentials (MSE) is Microsoft's latest system security offering. It is currently a free download for all "genuine" Windows systems. MSE offers antivirus and antimalware protection. MSE can dynamically update its virus signatures if it senses suspicious activity. MSE can also create system restore points before it cleans a system. This allows you to restore the system if there is a problem.

Credential Management

Credential management is an important part of system security. Nowadays, in order to ensure security, many sites are password protected. Passwords help prevent unwanted users from accessing confidential or private information. With the abundance of password-protected sites, users are finding it difficult to keep track of all these passwords. If you choose to store passwords, they must be stored in a secure manner so that they cannot be stolen.

Windows Credential Manager

Windows 7 provides Credential Manager to handle credential management. Credential Manager is used to store passwords for various sites in one place. Instead of remembering all these passwords, the user can simply store them in Credential Manager and have Windows submit the passwords to the appropriate site. These could be Web sites or network locations. The Credential Manager section of Control Panel has one option: Manage Windows credentials

Manage Windows Credentials

This option brings up the Credential Manager window, as shown in Figure 4.16. Credential Manager allows you to save Windows credentials, certificate-based credentials, and generic credentials. If you choose to save Windows or generic credentials, you will be prompted to enter the Internet or network address, the user name, and the password. If you choose to save certificate-based credentials, you will have to enter the Internet or network and select the appropriate certificate from your certificate store.

Credential Manager also gives you the ability to back up and restore your credential vault. This is useful if your credential vault becomes corrupted for any reason. Your vault backups will be protected with a password. This password must be supplied before a restore is allowed. This helps prevent unwanted users from accessing your credentials.

Figure 4.16 Credential Manager window.

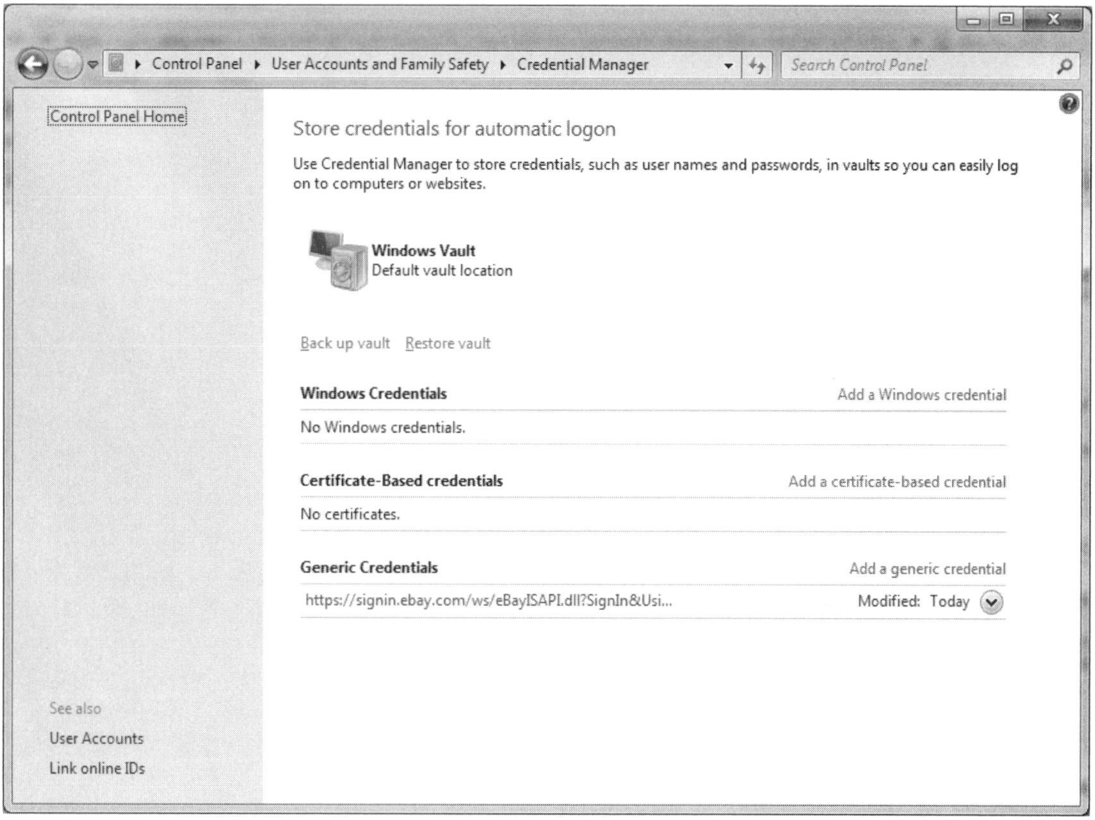

Summary

Some security threats are specific to your environment. But there are many threats out there that are dangerous in any environment. Any environment can be susceptible to viruses, Trojans, root kits, and privilege escalation. It's important that you take the necessary steps to protect your environment from these threats.

Your system protection should entail many layers. This is because system vulnerabilities exist at many layers. There are hardware, operating system, application, and peripheral device threats. Each type of threat requires a different defense and a different method of remediation. These threats have been further intensified by the adoption of virtualization. One of the key concerns with virtualization is where security should be done. You want to maintain security without causing so much of a resources burden that you lose some of the effectiveness of virtualization. Windows 7 and Windows Server 2008 R2 include a number of applications that help you secure your systems and protect against these threats.

ORGANIZATIONAL AND OPERATIONAL SECURITY

INFORMATION IN THIS CHAPTER

- Physical Security Concepts and Vulnerabilities
- Policies and Procedures
- Risk Analysis
- Business Continuity and Disaster Recovery

Other components of security mostly deal with technology. Organizational and operational security is mostly concerned with people, process, and procedures. The people within your organization can represent the biggest threat. These threats could be intentional and unintentional. You can use technology to enforce the processes and procedures, but a lot of it has to do with user education and training.

You need to ensure that employees know what to do in certain situations. Whether there's some sort of security incident or natural disaster, all employees need to understand their roles and responsibilities and the procedures they need to follow. Having a plan provides structure and helps prevent confusion and mistakes.

Physical Security Concepts and Vulnerabilities

Controlling physical access to systems is very important. Taking steps to prevent attackers from accessing your data over the network is useless if someone can just walk right up to the system and take the data. Physical security is about more than just security guards. It's about making sure that your systems are secure from internal and external threats.

Security for Microsoft Windows System Administrators. DOI: 10.1016/B978-1-59749-594-3.00005-3

Physical Access Control

Physical access control is just that—controlling who has physical access to your environment and your systems. Physical access control starts outside and extends all the way inside to the systems themselves. The access control systems you have in place need to uphold the access control policies your organization has put in place.

Perimeter

Fences represent the first line of security. Installing fences will help prevent unwanted individuals from simply walking onto your property. Depending on how the fences are installed, individuals may have to enter the property using a gate. If you are protecting a parking lot, the gate may be a barrier arm. A gate is much easier to secure than the entire property line. You can put a guard at the gate or use a badge system for entering or leaving the parking lot.

It's important to keep a clear perimeter. That means not letting trees and shrubs get overgrown or out of control. If the perimeter is clear, it is easy to monitor. It will make it easier to detect someone coming onto the premises. It will also make it easier to notice suspicious activity.

Security guards are also important. Sometimes just a physical presence is enough to deter intruders. Roving guards are generally effective in deterring malicious activity. Having a couple of roving guards is also generally less expensive than having many stationary guards stationed all over the facility.

Guarding your exterior helps not only with physical security but also with one particular network security vulnerability, war driving. War driving is when an attacker drives from parking lot to parking lot hoping to pick up a wireless network signal. Securing your parking lot can help prevent attackers from using your parking lot to search for a wireless signal.

Physical Barriers and Protection

Physical barriers are used to prevent and protect against unauthorized access to your environment. Of course, locked doors are used to prevent entry. But there are other physical barriers that can be used to protect and secure your environment.

You may have frosted glass that is used to prevent people from seeing things they shouldn't. You have to worry about not only people inside your company seeing but also people outside your company. Frost exterior windows can be used to prevent people external to your company from seeing confidential information you may have written on whiteboards or displayed on overhead projectors.

Surveillance cameras are useful for being able to monitor areas that you cannot be in physically. You cannot be everywhere at once, so having an efficient surveillance system can help keep your environment protected. You can monitor the entire environment from one central location. A good surveillance system also helps if there is some sort of incident. If your surveillance system records, you can replay the tape for when the incident occurred. This may give you clues about what really happened.

Computer Room Environment

Now that you have protected the external environment, it's time to move inside. This is where we will focus on the computer environment. Protecting the computer involves more than just physical security; there are other aspects that must be considered when protecting your computer environment.

Computer Room Entry

You must protect the entry to your computer room. Controlling who enters and leaves the room is essential in controlling who has physical access to the systems. You should have some method for limiting who can enter the computer room. Not only do you need to limit who can access the room, you should also limit who can grant access to the room. There should be a periodic review of the computer room access to ensure that it stays up-to-date.

Room entry can be limited using keyed entry or badge entry. Keyed entry is effective, but badge entry can be more robust. Badge entry tied to a computer system also gives you the ability to log who entered the room and when. An effective audit trail will help if an incident occurs. The problem with badge entry is that it's much more expensive to maintain than keyed entry, but if it fits within the budget, it would be preferable.

Temperature and Humidity

Temperature and humidity control is important for computer rooms. Excess heat can cause premature breakdown of the mechanical components of computer systems. You have to remember that the temperature of the systems themselves will always be higher than the room temperature. It's advisable to maintain a computer room temperature between 65 and 73 F. A lot of people know about the damage that excess heat can cause, but excess humidity can be just as dangerous. Excess humidity can cause corrosion of the metal used in some computer parts. You should generally maintain humidity between 40 and 50 percentages in your computer room.

Fire Suppression

Fire suppression is not just a good idea. It's required in most buildings. Fire suppression systems protect not only computer equipment but also personnel. And actually, personnel safety is more important than computer equipment safety. There are three main fire suppression system types: wet pipe systems, dry pipe systems, and chemical suppression systems.

Wet pipe systems are named thusly because the pipes in wet pipe systems are always filled with water. Even when the system has not been activated, the pipes are filled with water. Generally, there are activators or plugs on the sprinklers attached to the pipes. When the temperature in the room reaches a certain temperature, the activator is triggered or the plug melts. This causes the sprinklers to begin dispensing water.

In dry pipe systems, the pipes are not filled with water when the system is not activated. Instead, they are filled with pressurized air. When the system is activated, the pipes then fill with water and the sprinklers begin dispensing water. So why would you want a sprinkler system where the pipes are not filled with water? One reason might be that the pipes are running outside. In cold weather, the water in the pipes could freeze and cause the pipes to burst. Another reason is to preserve computer equipment. The water from your fire suppression system can ruin computer equipment. But some regulations require sprinklers to be installed everywhere in the building. This is mostly to protect personnel. With a dry system, you have more time before the sprinklers start dispensing water. In this time, you can deactivate the system and use some other method to put out the fire.

The final type of suppression system is a chemical system. Fires need oxygen in order to start, grow, or maintain themselves. Most chemical systems take advantage of this. Chemical systems will emit a chemical that will remove the oxygen from the room. Without oxygen, the fire will die. Chemical fire suppression systems are very effective where water-based systems are ineffective, like oil- or chemical-based fires. The problem is that when the oxygen is removed from the room, then personnel will also suffer from lack of oxygen. So, chemical systems should not be activated with personnel present.

Policies and Procedures

Your organizations' policies and procedures provide formal guidance for employees. Formal policies and procedures help to eliminate confusion about what is required. They help personnel to understand their role and what their responsibilities are. Good policies and procedures also help personnel to understand how certain security measures affect them.

Corporate Security Policy

Your corporate security is a comprehensive policy that should cover all security aspects within your organization. It's important to document this policy so that everyone knows what the security rules and regulations are for the company. Having the policy documented makes it easier to disseminate the information. It also makes it easier to enforce.

Your corporate security policy should contain an acceptable use policy. An acceptable use policy outlines the allowed usage of your network and systems. An acceptable use policy may outline what Web sites people can visit, what can be sent via e-mail, or what types of software people can install. When employees start at a company, they may be required to sign the acceptable use policy before they begin working.

An acceptable use policy not only helps to govern network and system usage but also provides a level of legal standing. For example, let's say Dale visited a Web site that had explicit material. Dale may claim that he was not aware that he was prohibited from visiting such sites at work and that he should not be punished. If Dale had signed an acceptable use policy that explained what was acceptable and what wasn't, he could not claim ignorance.

Your corporate security policy should also contain a nondisclosure agreement. A nondisclosure agreement helps to deter employees and others from sharing confidential company information with others. Violation of a nondisclosure agreement usually results in some sort of legal action seeking compensation for damages.

System Security Policy

You should have a system security policy that outlines required configurations and settings for computer systems. Your system security policy will dictate what software can and cannot be installed on systems. It will also specify certain software that may be required on all systems, like antivirus software. You will probably want to have different system security policies for servers,

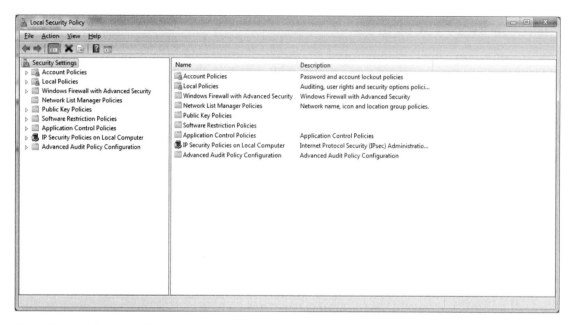

Figure 5.1 Local Security Policy application.

desktops, and laptops. There will be probably a lot of items common to all three, but there will definitely be differences also. For example, you may want to have a policy that prevents all users, except administrators, from logging onto server consoles.

Local Security Policy Application

Windows comes with tools, the aid in the implementation of your system security policy. One of these tools is the local security policy application, as shown in Figure 5.1. The Local Policies section of the local security policy application allows you to easily configure and enforce system settings.

User Rights Assignment: The User Rights Assignment section, as shown in Figure 5.2, allows you to assign system rights to various users and groups. You can control who can do what on the system. Some of the more widely used settings here are as follows:

- **Allow log on locally** This controls who can log onto the system console. On server systems, you will probably want to disable this for everyone except administrators.
- **Allow log on through Remote Desktop Services** This controls who can log onto the system using a Remote Desktop Services session. On workstations, you probably want only administrators to have this right on workstations. You will probably want to adjust it on servers running Remote Desktop Services that publish desktops or applications.

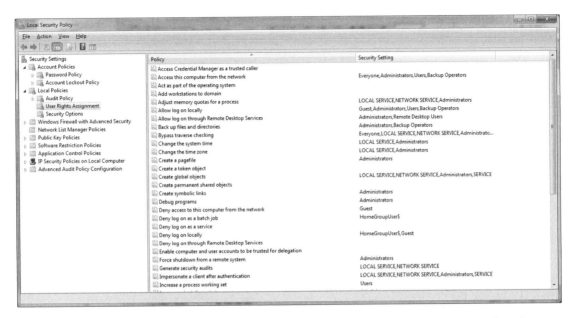

Figure 5.2 Local Security Policy – User Rights Assignment.

- **Shut down the system** This controls who can shut down the system. You will definitely want to restrict this right on servers.

Security Options: The Security Options section, as shown in Figure 5.3, allows you to configure security settings for the system. These settings apply no matter which user is logged into the system. Some of the more widely used settings here are as follows:

- **Audit: Shut down system immediately if unable to log security audits** This option will shut down the system if it cannot write to the security audit logs. This may happen if the logs have reached their size limit. You may want to set this option because if the system cannot write to the security logs, there is no way for you to audit what took place on the system.
- **Interactive logon: Do not display last user name** This option will prevent the system from showing the name of the user who last logged into the system. If multiple users log into a system, you may set this option for security or convenience.
- **Interactive logon: Message text for users attempting to log on** This option will display a message when users attempt to log into the system. You can make this a warning message discouraging unauthorized access to the system.

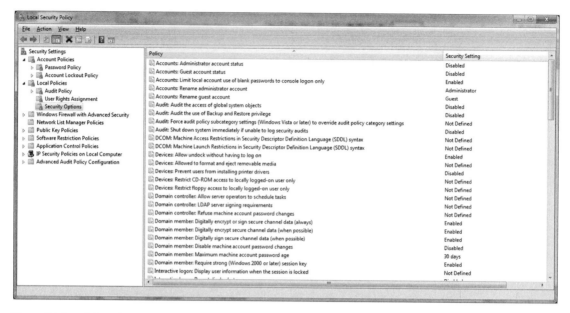

Figure 5.3 Local Security Policy – Security Options.

User Security Policy

The user security policy will outline how user accounts will be handled. It will discuss how user accounts will be created and what settings will be configured for user accounts. It will also dictate what information will be associated with user accounts.

Part of your user security policy may be to disable certain built-in accounts. Unused accounts represent a security risk. Unless it's enabled for a reason, you should start by disabling the Guest account. On Windows 7 and Windows Server 2008 R2 systems, the Guest account is disabled by default. The default Administrator account may represent vulnerability. If you are using the default Administrator account, an attacker knows of an account with administrator-level privileges that he or she can attack. You may want to disable or rename the default Administrator account. By default, Windows 7 systems have the default Administrator account disabled.

Group Policy Management Editor

The local security policy application will also help you to implement portions of your company's user security policy. You can configure user account settings and password policy settings. But if you want to configure these options for your domain, you will

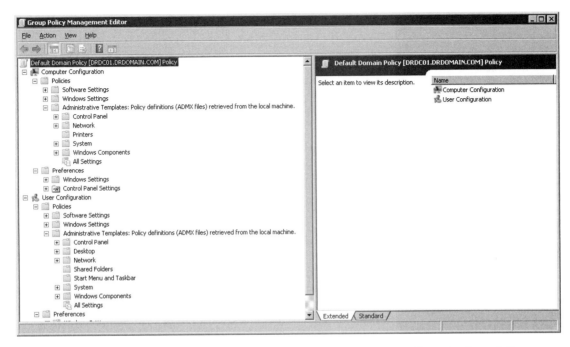

Figure 5.4 Group Policy Management Editor.

have to use the Group Policy Management Editor, as shown in Figure 5.4.

Password Policy: The Password Policy section, as shown in Figure 5.5, allows you to configure how passwords will be handled and restrictions around how passwords are set. This allows you to force users to create stronger passwords. This helps protect again password guessing attempts. The settings available here are as follows:

Enforce password history This option allows you to control how often passwords can be reused. On Windows Server 2008 R2 domain controllers, the default is 24 passwords.

Maximum password age This option specifies how long a user can go between password changes. The default on domain controllers is 42 days.

Minimum password age This option specifies how long a user must have a password before it can be changed. The default on domain controllers is 1 day.

Minimum password length This option specifies how long a user's password must be. The default on domain controllers is seven characters.

Password must meet complexity requirements This option sets requirements for what characters must be used in a password.

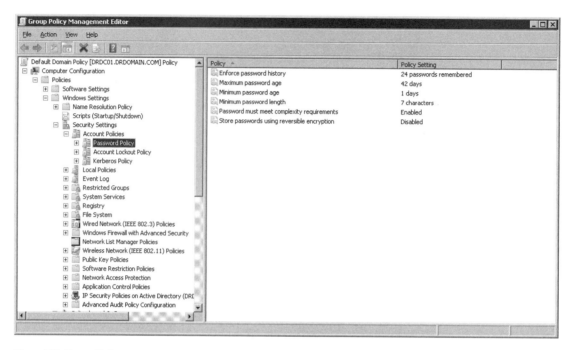

Figure 5.5 Group Policy Management Editor – Password Policy.

Store passwords using reversible encryption This option controls how passwords will be stored. Some applications need to be able to access passwords. This option will help allow this.

Account Lockout Policy: The Account Lockout section, as shown in Figure 5.6, allows you to configure account lockout settings. Account lockout allows you to lock an account after repeated failed login attempts. This helps protect against brute force password-cracking attempts. The settings available here are as follows:

- **Account lockout duration** This option controls how long an account will be locked out. By default, this option is disabled because account lockout is disabled.
- **Account lockout threshold** This option controls how many bad login attempts will cause an account to be locked. By default this option is disabled.
- **Reset account lockout counter after** This option controls how long the system will wait after the last unsuccessful attempt before it resets the lockout counter. By default, this option is disabled because account lockout is disabled.

Kerberos Policy (only available on domain controllers): The Kerberos Policy section, as shown in Figure 5.7, allows you to

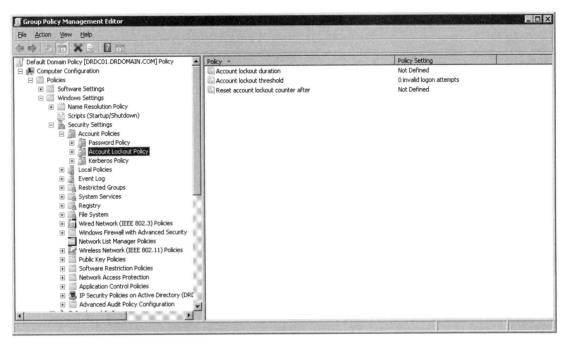

Figure 5.6 Group Policy Management Editor – Account Lockout.

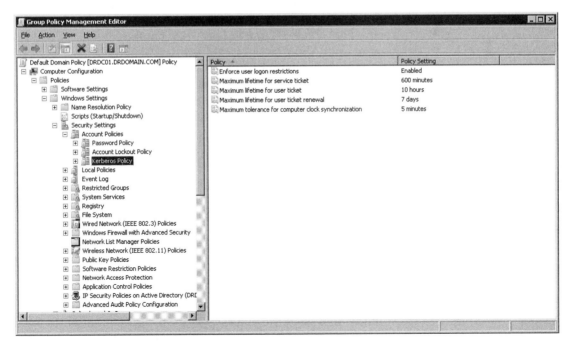

Figure 5.7 Group Policy Management Editor – Kerberos Policy.

configure how Kerberos will be handled in your domain. Kerberos is the default authentication method used in Windows 2008 R2 domains. The settings available here are as follows:

- **Enforce user logon restrictions** This option controls whether every session ticket request is checked against the user rights policy. This option is more secure, but it does take up extra network bandwidth. It is enabled by default.
- **Maximum lifetime for service ticket** This option controls how long service tickets will be valid. The default is 600 min.
- **Maximum lifetime for user ticket** This option controls how long user tickets will be valid. The default is 10 h.
- **Maximum lifetime for user ticket renewal** This option controls the timeframe for which a Ticket-Granting Ticket can be renewed. The default is seven days.
- **Maximum tolerance for computer clock synchronization** This option specifies the maximum difference in time that can exist between the client and the domain controller. This is to help prevent replay attacks. The default is five min.

Data Security Policy

Your company will have many different types of data. Some data will be more important than other data. Some data will be more confidential than other data. The rules you use to govern these types of data will be different. You have to take additional steps to secure data if that is more important or confidential.

The first thing you should start with is classifying your data into different categories. These categories should be based on importance and confidentiality. Once your data has been classified, then you can begin setting policies based on these classifications. For each classification, you should specify the following:

- Who will have access to the data?
- What can be done with the data?
- How will the data be stored?
- How will the data be transmitted?

Incident Response Policy

Computer-related incidents occur in every company. It doesn't always have to be stolen data. It could be a virus outbreak or a compromised system. It's important that everyone in the company knows what to do if one of these event occurs. This is what your incident response policy if for. It will outline everyone's roles and responsibilities with regard to an incident.

First Responders

The first responders are the first people on the scene when there is an incident. You need to do two things. First, you need to determine who the first responders will be. Then, you need to determine the roles and responsibilities of the first responders. For computer-related incidents, you will definitely want someone from the IT security team to respond. Depending on the nature of the incident, you may also need representatives from Human Resources or security guards to also respond. The very first thing that needs to be done is the incident needs to be verified. Someone needs to determine that an incident actually occurred and the nature of the incident.

Damage Control

Once an incident has been reported and the incident response team has been contacted, you then need to worry about damage control. You want to try to prevent further damage from being done. You should start by isolating the affected system or systems, especially if the incident involved some sort of malicious activity like the spreading of a virus. The systems should be disconnected from all wired or wireless networks. Any remote connections that can be made to or from the system should be disabled. Peripheral devices, especially modems, should be disconnected.

Preservation of Evidence

The next step is to make sure evidence is preserved properly. Improperly preserved evidence may be inadmissible if the incident requires legal action. The key is that you want to make sure that evidence is maintained in its original form. There are three very effective methods of preservation that should be used:

- **Capture memory and cache** If possible you should save the contents of the system memory, cache, and any other volatile memory locations.
- **Image systems** You should create an image or do a bit-level copy of the system hard drive.
- **Log activity** You should log all activity that occurs on the system after the incident.

In addition, you must refrain from restarting or powering computers on your own. The computers may have a mechanism in place that will delete evidence if the computer is started or restarted.

Chain of Custody

After evidence is collected, then you have to track the chain of custody. The chain of custody refers to who had custody for a piece of evidence. When investigating an incident, you must know who was in possession of the evidence at any given time. This is to ensure that the evidence was not tampered with or mishandled. You start by documenting how the evidence was collected and preserved. Then, you must document any changes in custody. Your documentation should include the following: who was in possession, how long they were in possession, why they were in possession, and signatures of all custodians.

Reporting

After all the evidence has been collected and the investigation has concluded, a report should be generated. The report should include a description of the incident, the evidence collected, and any conclusions that were made. If appropriate, it should also include any measures that will be taken to prevent a similar incident from occurring again. The report should be distributed to all relevant management personnel.

End User Education

Your end users play a large role in the security of your environment. End users are the ones who will follow and carry out a lot of rules and policies you have put in place. You need to make sure end users are aware of these rules and policies and what they mean. It's also helpful if they understand what the rules and policies mean to them.

End user education helps to reduce the amount of unintentional security incidents. Users know what they need to do, or not do, to prevent breaches or compromises. Education also helps to set expectations and establishes end user requirements. You are letting users know what is expected from them. You should also inform them of what can happen if they do not meet those expectations.

End user education can take many forms. End users should definitely be made aware of security policies and procedures during new user classes. This helps to start everything off on the right foot. But you can't just stop there. Educating users just once is not enough. You should make sure that they are given periodic refreshers of your company's security policies and procedures. Having required documentation reviews maybe once a year will help keep information fresh in everyone's mind. You also need to make sure that users are notified when policies and procedures change. This can be done through announcements and the use of tip sheets to help everyone understand what changes were made and why they made.

Social Engineering

Social engineering attacks are based on physical interactions. Social engineering attacks are more prevalent than most people think. The reason for their prevalence is that they are relatively easy to implement. Attackers attempt to convince someone to give them confidential information. This could be a username, a password, or the location of sensitive data. For example, let's look at the following conversation:

Phone rings

Christina: Hello, this is Christina.

Kim: Hi, Christina, this is Kim from the Help Desk.

Christina: Hi, Kim.

Kim: Christina, your password is about to expire and I have called to help you reset it. Some people have had trouble with theirs, so we are calling everyone to help them.

Christina: Ok. What do I need to do?

Kim: Just tell me your old password and the new password you would like to use, and I will set it for you.

Christina: My old password is Jay, and I want my new password to be Lauren.

Kim: Ok. It's all set. Thank you very much.

Christina: Thanks, Kim.

Kim: You're welcome

In this example, Christina gave Kim her password. As it turned out, Kim really wasn't from the Help Desk. She was an attacker who had been calling around to trick people into giving her their passwords. She had already gotten Briana's and Aiden's passwords.

This type of situation is not uncommon. Attackers may call on the phone pretending to be from the Help Desk. They may say that the user's password needs to be reset and the only way they can do that is for the user to give them her their old password. If the user needs persuasion, the attacker may threaten to call the employee's manager and tell him or her that the user is being uncooperative.

Attackers may also attempt to convince someone to provide them with access to a secured area. Let's say Patrick comes into work in the morning, and Rena from Accounting says she left her badge in her car and asks Patrick to let her in. Patrick obliges.

It seems harmless, but Patrick does not know that Rena was fired the day before.

Reverse Social Engineering: Many companies have started to educate their employees to prevent social engineering attacks. Employees are told to give out information only to qualified individuals. Because of this, a new form of social engineering called reverse social engineering was developed. In reverse social engineering, the attacker presents valid information to the user. This is done in an attempt to convince the user that the attacker is a "qualified individual." The hope is that the user will trust the attacker because the attacker was able to provide what the user thought was sensitive information, or is able to help the user with his or her problems.

Reverse social engineering attacks usually involve some type of sabotage, offering of help, and then assisting. Let's say Samia wants to perform a reverse social engineering attack on Rafael and Warren, both of whom handle sensitive accounting information. Samia may sabotage Rafael's and Warren's computers. Then, she may go to their desks and offer to help them. While fixing their computers, she may ask them for their passwords, which she plans to use later. The key with reverse social engineering attacks is to gain the user's confidence. Samia doesn't have to ask for confidential information right away. She can wait until a later date because she has already gained Warren's and Rafael's confidence.

Preventing Social Engineering Attacks

The main way to prevent social engineering attacks is through end user training. Employees must be trained how to act when certain situations arrive. This way, they are not caught off guard. Users should also be trained on what suspicious activity to look for. For example, if your company has a policy that says that Help Desk personnel will never ask for user passwords, then anyone claiming to be from the Help Desk who asks for a user's password should be reported.

Risk Analysis

Risk plays a huge role in security. In most cases, when you secure something, you are trying to mitigate some sort of risk of attack. There's also the fact that it's virtually impossible to completely secure everything. The cost would be outrageous, and usability would be minimal. So, you have to make some concessions. A good risk analysis process will help you determine what concessions should be made and where.

Asset Identification

The purpose of securing your organization is to protect your company's assets. You can't protect your assets unless you first know what they are. Assets can come in different forms: they can be tangible and or intangible. Some examples of assets you may want to protect are people, data, equipment, or services. Another valuable resource that is often overlooked is company reputation. Even though a security breach may not have a big direct impact, it could affect company reputation. If your company's reputation is soiled, you may have difficulty in attracting new business, or even maintain existing customers.

After you have identified your assets, you should assign a value to them. This value helps you determine what cost would be acceptable to secure the asset. In general, you don't want to spend more protecting an asset than it would cost you if the asset were lost.

Risk Assessment

A proper risk assessment will help you determine what areas of your environment are at risk. The results of the risk assessment will give you an idea where you should invest your time and money. In some cases, there may be vulnerability, but no risk. If there is no risk, you probably don't need to devote resources to mitigate a nonexistent risk. Some key areas where you might want to focus your risk assessment are authentication schemes, methods of access, and single points of failure.

Authentication Schemes

You should examine the authentication schemes used in your organization. Some authentication mechanisms are more secure than others. You should look at how credentials are stored and how they are transmitted. You should consider how easily replay attacks or man-in-the-middle attacks could be performed.

Methods of Access

The different methods of access used by your organization can present a multitude of issues. One of the key concerns here would be remote access. You must remember that remote access does not require a user's physical identity to be verified. In order for someone to access your local wired network, his or her physical identity must be verified when that person enters the building. This is not true of remote access. With remote access, there is almost no way to verify for sure who is on the other end of the line.

Single Points of Failure

You examine your environment to search for any single points of failure. Single points of failure not only open you up to denial-of-service attacks, but they also represent potential risks in case of natural disasters. Any identified single point of failure should be corrected if possible. If not, you should make sure that you properly monitor these areas so that you may be able to predict and hopefully prevent a failure.

Vulnerabilities

After you have identified your assets and discovered your risk areas, you need to check your systems for vulnerabilities. Vulnerability is a flaw or weakness that could potentially be exploited by an attacker. You should check all your systems for vulnerabilities, but you should focus a bulk of your efforts on systems you have identified as risks. Most software vendors will publicly report vulnerabilities in their applications. But you still need to do testing of your own to discover additional vulnerabilities in the applications themselves or in your implementation of the applications. There are two types of testing that could be used: blind testing and knowledgeable testing.

Blind Testing

Blind testing is done assuming that you have no knowledge of the organization's systems or applications. Blind testing is done using a generic set of test cases. Blind testing gives you a sense of what would be discovered from a typical attacker who does not have internal knowledge of your company. You test different systems and different areas, trying to discover vulnerabilities and find information.

Knowledgeable Testing

In knowledgeable testing, testing is performed using knowledge of the systems and infrastructure of the company. This is the type of knowledge an external attacker generally would not have. But internal attackers may have this knowledge. Knowledgeable testing is generally more focused than blind testing because you know certain areas where your efforts may yield better results.

Business Continuity and Disaster Recovery

Maintaining the day-to-day operations of your company is crucial. Occasionally, events will occur that make this difficult. Systems will fail, security breaches will occur, and natural disasters will happen.

These types of events will test whether you have properly planned for and mitigated risks. Your business continuity and disaster recovery planning could make or break your company. Many companies cannot afford two or three days of downtime. You need to make sure that business can proceed in these trying circumstances.

Service-Level Agreements

Service-level agreements (SLAs) are agreements between a service provider and a consumer as to what the consumer can expect from the provider. Often, these agreements are contractual, and some penalty can be imposed if these requirements are not met. With external providers these are easier to enforce. Failure to meet an SLA might carry a financial penalty or result in cancellation of a contract. It gets a little trickier when you deal with internal providers. Failure to adhere to an SLA internally generally results in an indirect penalty. For example, failure to adhere to SLAs may result in a negative performance appraisal, which may lead to some other penalty.

Setting SLAs is a multistep process. You begin by identifying critical systems. These are usually systems that have a direct impact on employee production or company profitability. These could be authentication systems, licensing systems, or order processing systems. Downtime in these systems would be a problem, and system degradation may also be a serious problem.

Next, you must determine acceptable service levels for these systems. You should define metrics for response time and system availability. You should also have SLAs covering when systems go down. There should be SLAs around recovery methods and recovery times. Sometimes a service will be delivered by a combination of systems. In this case, there should be SLAs for the individual systems and a composite SLA for the combination of systems.

Finally, there should be established penalties for when SLAs are violated. Ideally, the severity of these penalties would be proportional to the severity of the violation. For external providers, a violation could result in a return of a portion of the service costs. Repeated violations could result in a cancellation of the service contract. You don't want to be stuck in a contract with a provider that repeatedly misses SLAs with no penalty. For internal providers, violations could result in negative performance appraisals. This may affect raises and bonuses for the individuals responsible.

High Availability and Fault Tolerance

High availability and fault tolerance are used to keep your systems running. Just because a component fails, that doesn't mean the whole system should fail. There are several different methods and tools you can use to keep a system going in spite of components failing. These range from application-level solutions to hardware-level solutions. Some of the most commonly used options are database replication and Windows Network Load Balancing.

Database Replication

Database replication can be used to provide fault tolerance that have a database back end. Database replication is relatively inexpensive to implement. You don't need specialized hardware or software. You just need to make sure that your database platform supports it. You also need to make sure that the application stores data in a way that is conducive to replication. In database replication, data is automatically copied from one database to another. In database replication, there is generally a publisher and a subscriber. The publisher is the database that holds the main copy of the data. The subscriber gets information by copying data from the publisher.

Windows Network Load Balancing

Windows Network Load Balancing (Windows NLB) is a feature built into Windows Server 2008 R2. Windows NLB allows for load balancing and fault tolerance. With Windows NLB, you have multiple systems online processing requests. Each system has its own IP address, but it shares a second IP address called a virtual IP. When a network request is sent to the virtual IP, Windows NLB will automatically load balance the request between the servers. If one of the servers goes down, the requests are sent to the remaining online servers. Windows Network Load Balancing does not require any special hardware other than a network card that supports the feature. You do have to make sure that the application being served supports load balancing and determine what type of load balancing it supports.

Backup and Restore

Backups are used to save your files and data. If there is an emergency or some sort of data loss, these files can be restored from your back ups. Designing your backup strategy is an important part of your business continuity and disaster recovery planning. First you have to decide what you want to back up. The most crucial items to back up are the ones that cannot be easily replaced, like data and configuration files. Then, you must decide what backup method you want to use. Each type of backup method has its own advantages and disadvantages. You should also make sure that you periodically test your backup process and your backups by attempting to do a restore. After all, your backups are worthless if they cannot be restored successfully.

Backup Methods

There are several characteristics that differentiate different backup methods. One of these is the archive bit. The archive bit is an attribute on a file or folder that is used to denote whether the file or folder has changed since the last backup of that file or folder was performed. Some backup methods set the archive bit; some do not. When deciding what type of backup method to use, you should consider the time it takes to do a backup. Some backup methods take longer than others. Remember, however, that in many cases your system will not be able to service requests properly while the backup is running. Recovery time is also an important consideration. When your data has been lost or your systems are down, speed of recovery is of the essence.

Full Backups

Full backups, sometimes called normal backups, are the most common type of backup. Full backups back up all files on the target system. Full backups reset the archive bit. Full backups generally take the longest to perform, because they back up all files. Full backups are generally the fastest to restore because all the files come from a single backup source.

Copy Backups

Copy backups are similar to full backups in the sense that copy backups back up all files on the target system. The difference is that copy backups do not reset the archive bit. Copy backups take the same amount of time to restore as full backups.

Differential Backups

Differential backups are usually used in combination with full backups. Differential backups will only back up all files that have the archive bit set. Because of this they will take a shorter amount of time to perform than full backups or copy backups. Differential backups do not reset the archive bit. So basically, every time you perform a differential backup you will be backing up every file that changed since the last full backup was performed. Complete restores using differential backups will generally take longer to perform than full backup restores because you will have to restore both the last full backup and the last differential backup.

Incremental Backups

Incremental backups are also usually used in combination with full backups. Incremental backups will only back up files that have the archive bit set. The difference between incremental backups and differential backups is that incremental backups reset the archive bit. This means that incremental backups will only backup files that have changed since the last full or incremental backup. This generally makes incremental backups quicker than differential backups. Complete restores with incremental backups, however, will take longer than restores with differential backups. This is because you will have to restore the last full backup and all the incremental backups that have occurred since that full backup.

Windows Backup

Windows 7 provides Windows Backup to allow you to perform backups and restores of your system. Windows backup is accessed through the Control Panel. In the **System and Security** section, click **Back up your computer**. This will launch the Backup and Restore window, as shown in Figure 5.8. You can use the Backup and Restore window to create a system image, create a system repair, or to perform a backup of your system.

The **back up now** option will start a new backup of your system. The backup will use your current backup device/location. The **turn**

Figure 5.8 Backup and Restore window.

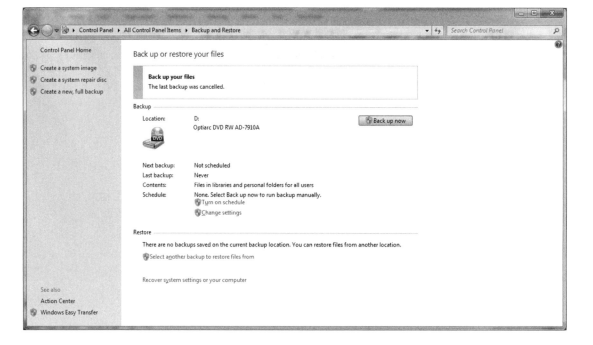

on schedule option will allow you to set up periodic backups of your system. You should schedule these backups for a time when the system will be online, but not in use. The **Change settings** option will allow you to change the default settings for your backups. You can use this to change the default backup location, for example.

If you need to perform a restore, use the **Select another backup to restore files from** option. This will bring up the Restore Files wizard. The Restore Files Wizard will walk you through doing a restore. You will have to specify the location of the backup to restore from, the files you want to restore, and what you want to do with the restored files.

Windows System Restore

The Windows System Restore application allows you to do complete restores or "point-in-time" restores of your Windows system. The Windows system Restore application is launched by selecting **System Restore** under Programs > Accessories > System Tools. This will launch the System Restore Wizard. The System Restore Wizard will allow you to select a restore point, as shown in Figure 5.9. Windows 7 will restore your system to the state it was at when the restore point was created. Windows 7 restore points will allow you to restore system files and settings without losing your personal files and data.

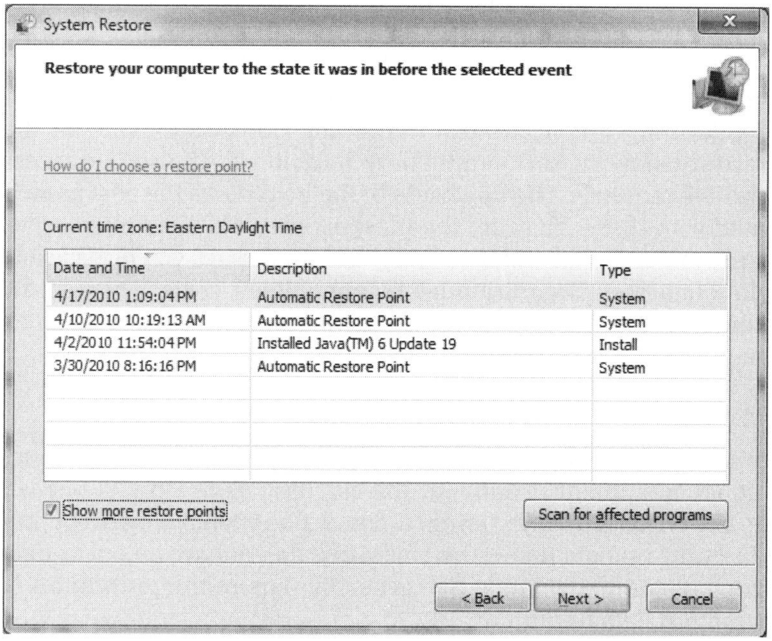

Figure 5.9 Restore point selection window.

The Recovery window also includes an option for Advanced Recovery Methods. These Advanced Recovery Methods will restore your system, but everything will be replaced, including your personal files and data. You can restore your system using a previously created image. You can also choose to reinstall Windows 7 using the installation media. If you choose either of these methods, you are given the option to back up your important files and data.

Alternate Sites

One way to ensure your company is able to continue business in the event of a disaster is through the use of an alternate site. An alternate site is a site that can be used by employees to continue working if their home site is down. Alternate sites should be a safe distance away from your company office. This way you can ensure the same disaster that affected your company's facilities did not affect the alternate facility. There are companies that offer alternate site services. You can simply rent space in one of their facilities. In some cases you could use one of your company's office locations as an alternate site for another location. As long as the location has sufficient capacity, this could help save your company money.

Hot Site

A hot site is a disaster recovery site that is up and running at all times. The site contains the infrastructure and systems needed to continue business activities. It also contains the latest copy of company data. This is generally achieved by using some sort of replication to replicate data to the site. Hot sites provide for the fastest failover. Users simply have to report to the site or access the site remotely. The downside of the hot sites is the cost associated with them. They are the most expensive type of alternative. In some cases, in order to maintain a hot site, you're basically doubling your organization's IT operational costs. This is why some companies choose to use remote office locations as alternate hot sites for other locations.

Warm Site

Warm sites are similar to hot sites. They usually have fully functional equipment running at the site. Very little work is needed to get systems up and running. The main difference between hot and warm sites is that warm sites often do not have an up-to-date copy of company data. They generally require the restoration of the latest data backup.

Cold Site

Cold sites range from having very little equipment to having no equipment at all. A cold site can simply be an empty warehouse or office space. Failover to a cold site requires that infrastructure be set up, systems configured, and data restored from backup. Cold sites are the least expensive alternate sites to maintain. The big disadvantage of cold sites is the time it takes to failover. Of all the alternate site types, cold sites take the longest to get up and running. This is due to the amount of work it takes to get the infrastructure in place and the systems configured. So you will have to weigh the cost against the recovery time.

Summary

The nontechnical aspects of security are just as, and in some cases, more important than technical aspects. There is no need to secure the data on a system if the system itself can be stolen. There is no need to set passwords if users will freely give their passwords to anyone. You have to make sure your physical location and the employees who work there don't represent a weakness in your security model.

Formalized policies and procedures are crucial in ensuring that employees understand and follow the security guidelines you have put in place. An end user education program helps to drive home the key themes and message of your security policy. After all, what good are policies and procedures if no one knows about them?

No matter how hard you plan, there will be security-related incidents. They could be big or small. But you must have a plan for dealing with them. If you don't have a plan, a relatively small incident could have a huge impact on your organization. Once you have developed your plan, you need to make sure that you test your plan. A plan that doesn't work, is just as bad as not having a plan at all. If your organization is unable to operate for too long, it could cease being a viable business institution. It may sound a little drastic, but it can happen.

SECURITY ASSESSMENTS AND AUDITS

INFORMATION IN THIS CHAPTER

- Vulnerability Assessments and Testing
- Monitoring
- Logging and Auditing

Just because you have taken steps to secure your environment doesn't mean that your job is done. You shouldn't just stop there. You need to make sure that the security measures you have put in place are effective and sufficiently protect your network and your systems. Periodic testing of your environment can help to give you the confidence that your environment is indeed secure. In addition, you need to periodically check what's going on in your environment. The quicker you notice suspicious activity, the sooner you can take action to prevent damage. Monitoring, auditing, and logging help you to get a better idea of what's going on with your network and your systems.

Vulnerability Assessments and Testing

You need to periodically check your environment to ensure that it is secure. Vulnerability assessments and testing can help to give you a better idea how secure your environment really is. Every day, vulnerabilities are discovered in software and hardware. In order to keep your systems secure, you have to install patches for these vulnerabilities. Vulnerability assessments will allow you to get an idea of which vulnerabilities have been patched and which haven't.

Security for Microsoft Windows System Administrators. DOI: 10.1016/B978-1-59749-594-3.00006-5

Port Scanning

Port scanning is used to determine what ports a system may be listening on. This will help an attacker to determine what services may be running on the system. Some port scanners scan through ports in numeric order; some use a random order. There are many different methods used for port scanning, including SYN scanning, ACK scanning, and FIN scanning.

Portsweeping is similar to port scanning. Portsweeping attempts to find listening ports on systems. The difference is that instead of scanning one system on multiple ports, with portsweeping, multiple systems are scanned on the same port. For example, if you want to exploit a particular SQL vulnerability, you need to find which systems are running SQL Server. You can use portsweeping to scan a network for systems that can potentially be exploited.

Network Mapping

Network mapping tools are used to map out your network topology. Network mapping tools can tell you what devices and systems exist on your network and where they are located. Some network mapping tools require the network to be manually diagrammed; some do auto-discovery. With auto-discovery, network components are automatically discovered, and connections are automatically diagramed. Some popular network mapping tools are Nmap, HP OpenView, and Whats Up Gold.

Penetration Testing

Penetration testing, sometimes called pen testing, is the process of attempting to find and exploit vulnerabilities in your environment. Penetration testing is done to give you an idea of not only the vulnerabilities that exist, but more importantly, what damage could be done if these vulnerabilities were exploited.

Penetration testing requires specialized skills that are generally not present in most organizations. Because of this, most companies tend to outsource penetration testing. When outsourcing penetration testing, you should make sure that the consultants perform not only blind testing but also knowledgeable testing. Knowledgeable testing is needed to help protect against internal threats and threats from ex-employees.

At the end of a penetration testing project, the results need to be posted. Penetration testing results should include not only the vulnerabilities found but also recommendations for fixes. The results should be circulated to the security team, business owners, and upper-level management. Decisions will need to be made about how the vulnerabilities found will be dealt with. This will depend on the cost of mitigation and the value of the asset being protected.

Monitoring

Monitoring allows you to get real-time information about what's happening in your environment. There are two main types of monitoring to be considered here: system monitoring and network monitoring. The tools used in these two types of monitoring are different, but the goals are the same. You want to find out about any suspicious activity occurring in your environment.

One very important concept to consider when monitoring systems is baselining. Baselines help you to define system levels during normal activity. It's very difficult for you to determine abnormal activity when you don't know what represents normal activity. For example, just because network utilization is high, that doesn't mean there is a virus loose on the network. Utilization on your network might always be high. This could be due to the fact that you need to increase network capacity, not that there is malicious activity occurring on the network.

System Monitoring

System monitoring allows you to monitor local system resources. This includes processor usage, memory, hard drive usage, network adapter usage, and other system resources. Oftentimes, when a system is infected with a virus, you might see high processor usage or high network adapter usage. This may be caused by the system trying to find other files or other systems to infect. System monitoring can also be used to determine what processes are running on a system. You can check systems for processes that are known for malicious activity. System monitoring can also help to point out single points of failure, or components that are at risk of a denial-of-service attack. For example, if your system always has high memory usage, someone could easily cause a denial of service by sending enough requests to increase the memory usage to capacity.

System Monitoring Tools

System monitoring tools can vary from operating system to operating system. They offer different features and monitor different system aspects. Some system monitoring tools require that each system be monitored separately. Some allow you to integrate monitoring of multiple systems into one console. Two commonly used tools that come with Windows 7 and Windows Server 2008 are Performance Monitor and Resource Monitor.

Task Manager

Task Manager is a quick and easy application built into Windows 7 and Windows Server 2008 R3. It is used to monitor system resources. Task Manager is especially helpful in finding malicious processes and potential denial-of-service attacks.

- **Applications** The Applications tab, as shown in Figure 6.1, allows you to view the status of applications running on the system. From this tab, you can end the task or create a dump file for the application.
- **Processes** The Processes tab, as shown in Figure 6.2, allows you to view information on processes running on your system.

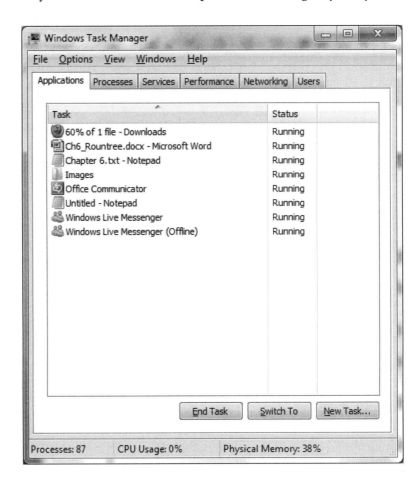

Figure 6.1 Task Manager – Applications tab.

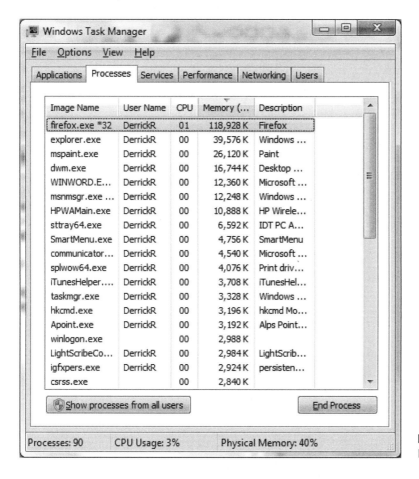

Figure 6.2 Task Manager – Processes tab.

You can view process names, memory used, handles used, and much more. From this tab, you can also terminate processes.

- **Services** The Services tab, as shown in Figure 6.3 shows all the services running on the system, their status, and the user used to run the service. You can also start and stop services from this tab.
- **Performance** The Performance tab, as shown in Figure 6.4, will show you overall resource usage on your system. You can view whether your system is short on memory or if the processor is spiking.
- **Networking** The Networking tab, as shown in Figure 6.5, will show you the usage statistics for your network adapters.
- **Users** The Users tab, as shown in Figure 6.6, will show which users are logged in locally or remotely to your system. From here, you can send messages to users, disconnect users, or log users off.

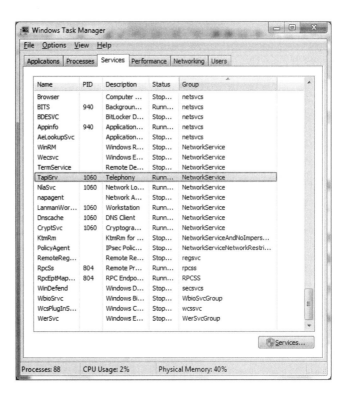

Figure 6.3 Task Manager – Services tab.

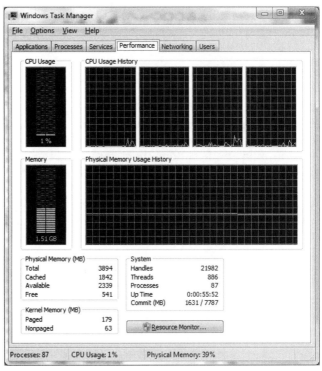

Figure 6.4 Task Manager – Performance tab.

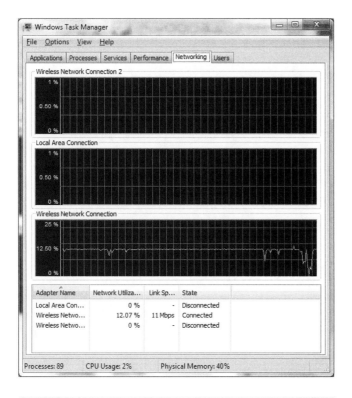

Figure 6.5 Task Manager – Networking tab.

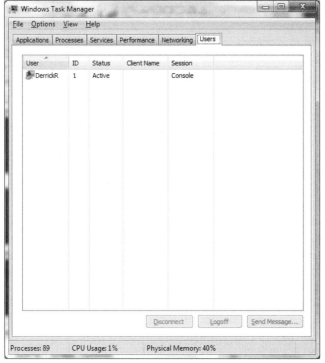

Figure 6.6 Task Manager – Users tab.

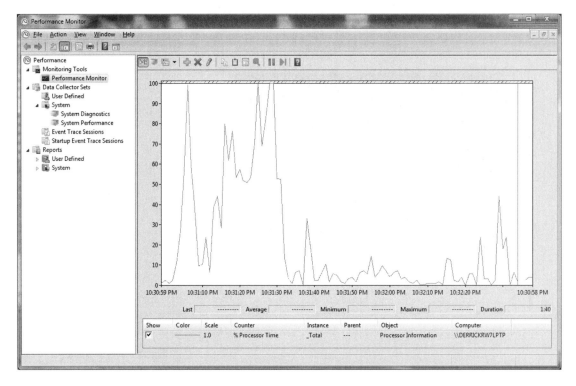

Figure 6.7 Performance
Monitor.

Performance Monitor

Performance Monitor, as shown in Figure 6.7, is available
from the Start Menu under Programs > Administrative Tools.
Performance Monitor allows you to view real-time activity or
to log activity. Performance Monitor uses performance counters, event trace data, and configuration information settings to
determine what to log and monitor. Performance counters show
system usage and activity, like memory usage, processor usage,
and so on. Event trace data is taken from trace providers on the
OS and in applications. Configuration information specifies
which registry keys to pull information from.

Performance Monitor uses Data Collector Sets to group what
information to gather. Performance Monitor includes two built-
in Data Collector Sets. They are System Diagnostics and System
Performance. You can also create your own.

To create your own Data Collector Set, do the following:

1. Under Data Collector Sets, right-click **User Defined** and select
   New > **Data Collector Set.** This will bring up the Create new
   Data Collector Set wizard, as shown in Figure 6.8.

2. As shown in Figure 6.8, Give your Data Collector a name and choose where to create one manually or use a template. We will use a template for this example. Click **Next**.
3. Choose which template you want to use. For this example, we will use the basic template, as shown in Figure 6.9. Click **Next**.

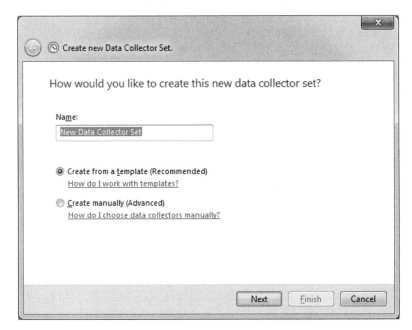

Figure 6.8 Create new Data Collector Set Wizard.

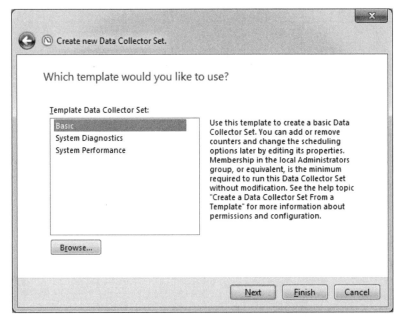

Figure 6.9 Performance Monitor data collector set template.

4. As shown in Figure 6.10, Choose where you would like to save Performance Monitor data for the Data Collector Set. Click **Next**.

5. As shown in Figure 6.11, Choose the account you want to use to run the Data Collector and whether you want to start the collection now. We will use the default account and start the collection now.

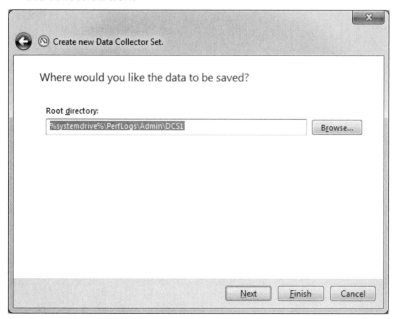

Figure 6.10 Data Collector Set Storage location.

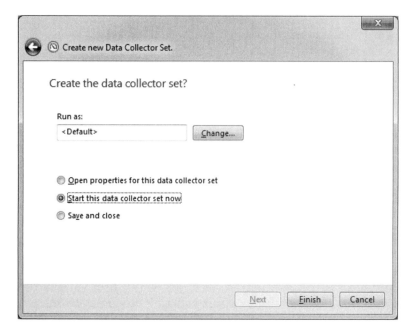

Figure 6.11 Start new Data Collector Set window.

The Data Collector Set will now appear under the User Defined section. You can open the new Data Collector Set to find and edit what Performance Counter, Configuration, and Kernel Trace settings are being used.

Resource Monitor

Resource Monitor can be used for tracking suspicious activity, troubleshooting, or for just figuring out what can be done to fine-tune your system and increase performance. Using Resource Monitor is easy. It can be accessed by running *resmon.exe* from the Search programs and files window or the Run window. Resource Monitor will show information about processes, services, and certain hardware devices. Throughout Resource Monitor, you have the ability to start, stop, and restart processes. You also have the ability to suspend processes, resume processes, end processes, and end process trees.

Resource Monitor groups the information it displays in order to make it easier to understand. There are five tabs in Resource Monitor: Overview, CPU, Memory, Disk, and Network. Each tab provides useful information for seeing what's going on with your system.

Resource Manager Overview Tab: The Overview tab of Resource Monitor, as shown in Figure 6.12, gives you a general overview of what is happening in your system. If you want more detailed information than what is given in the sections on the Overview tab, you have to go to the other tabs. There are four sections on the Overview tab: CPU, Disk, Network, and Memory.

- **CPU** The CPU section of the Overview tab gives information on processes running on the system. You can find out process IDs, the number of threads used, CPU consumption, and the average percentage of CPU consumption. This can help you to determine if a process is hogging the CPU's memory.
- **Disk** The Disk section of the Overview tab gives information on disk activity. You can see which processes are using the disk. You can see read rates and write rates. This can help you to determine if a process is causing excessive disk usage.
- **Network** The Network section of the Overview tab gives information about network activity. It shows processes, the network address they are connected to, bytes sent, and bytes received. This can help you to determine if a process is flooding the network.
- **Memory** The Memory section of the Overview gives information about memory usage on the system. It will tell you the working set and private bytes used by each process. It will also tell you if processes are generating hard faults. You can use

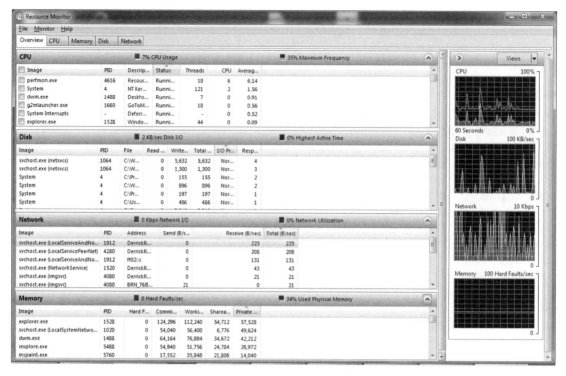

Figure 6.12 Resource Monitor – Overview tab.

this information to tell you if a process is leaking memory or if you need to add memory to your system.

Resource Monitor CPU Tab: The Resource Monitor CPU tab, as shown in Figure 6.13, provides detailed CPU usage information. You can get CPU information services and processes running on the system. In the pane on the right, you can view total CPU usage or CPU usage per processor. It helps to know if one CPU is being pegged. This generally means there is some misbehaving or malicious service or process utilizing your resources.

The Resource Monitor CPU tab has four sections: Processes, Services, Associated Handles, and Associate Modules. Each of these sections can help you in different ways. A lot of times you might have to use information from multiple sections to figure out what the true issue is.

- **Processes** The Process section of the CPU tab provides the same information shown in the CPU section of the Overview tab. It gives you a good overview of what's happening with the CPU in your system. You can see the process ID, description, status, threads, percentage of CPU usage, and average CPU usage for processes running on the system.

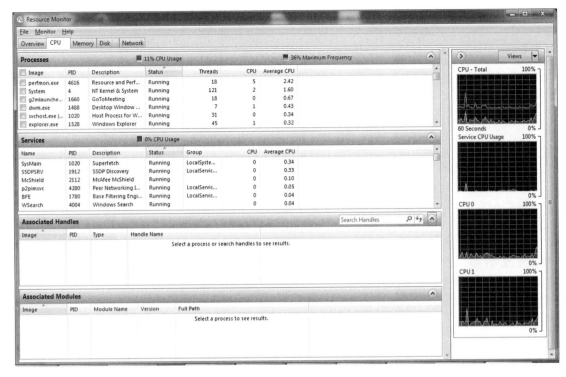

Figure 6.13 Resource Monitor – CPU tab.

- **Services** The Services section of the CPU tab gives you information on what processing resources are being used by the services running on your system. You can see service name, process ID, service description, service status, service group, percentage of CPU usage, and average CPU usage.
- **Associated Handles** The Associated Handles section gives you information on what handles are being used by various processes. The Associated Handles section is empty until you select a process in the Process section of this tab. This section will tell you the type of handle and the handle name for each handle used by the selected process.
- **Associated Modules** The Associated Modules section gives you information on which modules are used by a given process. Like the Associated Handles section, the Associated Modules section is empty until you select a process in the Process section of this tab. The Associated Modules section will tell you the module name, version, and path for the modules used by the selected process.

Resource Monitor Memory Tab: The Resource Monitor Memory tab, as shown in Figure 6.14, provides detailed memory

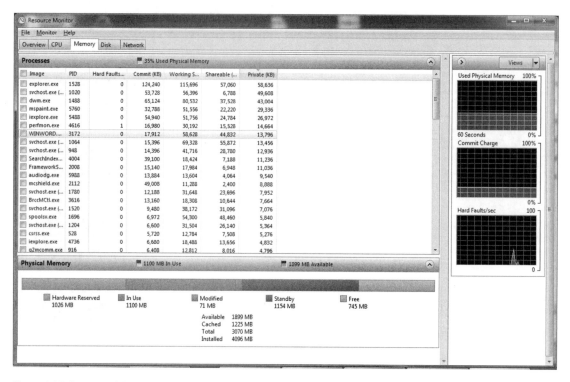

Figure 6.14 Resource Monitor – Memory tab.

usage information. You can get memory information for the processes running on the system. In the pane on the right, you can view the total amount of physical memory used by the system, the commit charge for the system, and the total number of hard page faults committed per second on the system. This information can help you to determine if you need to add more physical memory to the system.

The Resource Monitor Memory tab has two sections: Processes and Physical Memory. Each section provides different information to help you troubleshoot your memory issues. One section focuses on individual processes; the other focuses on the entire system.

- **Processes** The Processes section of the Memory tab gives information on memory usage for each process. This tab shows the same information as the Memory section of the Overview tab. You can see process name, process ID, hard faults/second, committed bytes, working set, shareable bytes, and private bytes for the processes running on the system.
- **Physical Memory** The Physical Memory section of the Memory tab gives information on physical memory usage in the system. This section will tell you the total amount of memory in

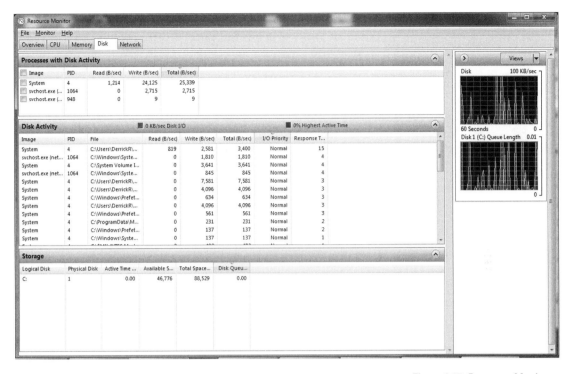

Figure 6.15 Resource Monitor – Disk tab.

the system, the total amount of memory available to the operating system, the amount of memory in use, and the amount of free memory. Depending on the operating system used and whether it's 32-bit or 64-bit, all of the memory in the system may not be available to the operating system.

Resource Monitor Disk Tab: The Resource Monitor Disk tab, as shown in Figure 6.15, provides information on disk usage on the system. In the right pane, you can see disk activity and disk queue length. This can help you to determine if your disks are processing requests fast enough, or if you need to do something to increase disk speed.

The Resource Monitor Disk tab has three sections: Processes with Disk Activity, Disk Activity, and Storage. These sections provide information on individual process and overall disk usage.

- **Processes with Disk Activity** The Processes with Disk Activity section of the Resource Monitor tab gives you information on disk usage by the processes running on the system. This section does not give individual disk access per process, but overall usage per process. Many times a single process can access the disk in multiple ways. This is not shown here. You can see process name, process ID, reads/second, writes/second, and total bytes/second.

- **Disk Activity** This Disk Activity section of the Resource Monitor Disk tab gives the same information as the Disk section of the Overview tab. This section gives information on individual disk access per process. You can see what each process is accessing on the disks. You can see process name, process ID, reads/second, writes/second, total bytes/second, I/O priority, and response time.
- **Storage** The Storage section of the Resource Monitor Disk tab gives information on overall disk usage. Information is given per logical volume. You can see which physical drive each logical drive resides on. You can also see active time, available space, total space, and disk queue length for each logical drive.

Resource Monitor Network Tab: The Resource Monitor Network tab, as shown in Figure 6.16, gives information on network activity on the system. You can view network usage information, connection information, and port information. In the right pane, you can see total network usage, number of TCP connections, local LAN usage, and wireless network usage. This can help you to figure out if a network bottleneck is occurring on a specific network or all networks.

The Resource Monitor Network tab provides detailed information on what's happening with your network connections.

Figure 6.16 Resource Monitor – Network tab.

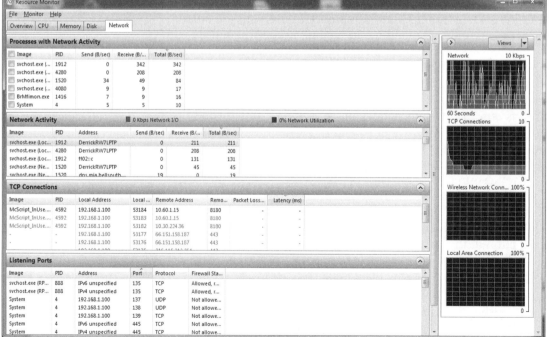

You can use this information to troubleshoot connection issues or port conflicts. The Resource Monitor Network tab has four sections: Processes with Network Activity, Network Activity, TCP Connections, and Listening Ports.

- **Processes with Network Activity** The Processes with Network Activity section of the Network tab gives general network activity information. You can see the processes that are running, process ID, bytes sent, bytes received, and total bytes. This can help you to determine if a process is generating excess network activity.

- **Network Activity** The Network Activity section provides the same information that's found in the Network section of the Overview tab. You can see process name, process ID, remote address, sent bytes, received bytes, and total bytes. You can use this information to determine what remote systems your system is communicating with, and how much data is being sent between the two systems.

- **TCP Connections** The TCP Connections section of the Network tab shows active TCP connections. You can see what remote systems you are connected to and what TCP ports are being used. This section shows process name, process ID, local address and port, remote address and port, packet loss, and latency. The information in this section can help troubleshoot dropped connections, which are often a result of high latency and/or packet loss.

- **Listening Ports** The Listening Ports section of the Network tab gives you information about the services and processes on your system that are waiting to service network requests. These services are listening on either a TCP or a UDP port. This section shows process name, process ID, listening address, port, protocol, and firewall status. The Listening Port section of the Network tab can come in very handy. It can tell you what ports a given service is listening on. This is very useful if you are trying to figure out why a given service is not accepting requests. It can also help you to resolve port conflicts. You may be trying to configure a service to start on a particular port, but keep getting a message about the port being in use. You can use the Listening Ports section to determine what service may be using the port you are trying to configure the new service with.

Network Monitoring

Network monitoring allows you to view activity on your network. You can look for excess network activity. Excess network activity can signal virus or worm activity. Network monitoring can help you not only identify excess network activity but also locate the source of the network traffic. In addition, knowing your network utilization and properly managing it can help you protect against denial-of-service attacks.

Network Monitoring Tools

There are a wide variety of network tools out there. Some can allow you to monitor all network activity occurring on your network. Some allow you to monitor only activity that flows through the system running the monitor. Microsoft provides Microsoft Network Monitor, which can be used to monitor network activity.

Microsoft Network Monitor

Microsoft Network Monitor, as shown in Figure 6.17, can be downloaded from the Microsoft Web site. Network Monitor allows you to capture and examine network traffic flowing through your network. Network Monitor allows you to choose which network interface you want to use to collect network traffic. This is especially useful if your system contains multiple interfaces. Network Monitor also includes a wide variety of parsers and parsing options to filter network traffic to make it easier to capture and examine.

Figure 6.17 Microsoft Network Monitor.

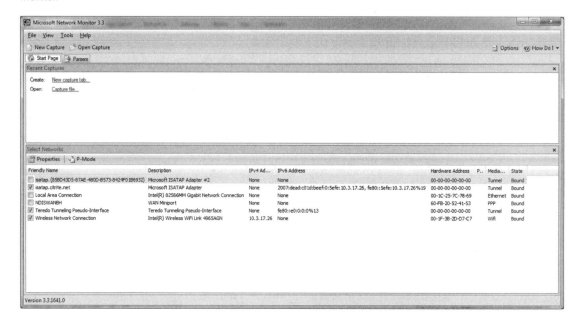

Logging and Auditing

Logging and auditing are key parts of your security architecture. Logging and auditing allow you review what has happened within your system over a period of time. It's important to know who did what and why on your systems. This can help you to differentiate normal activity from malicious activity.

Logging

There are many different types of logs. You can have hardware or system logs, operating system logs, application logs, and security logs, just to name a few. With all these types of logs, you need to have a policy that details what will and won't be logged. You need to determine whether you will log when access is granted or just when access is denied. Logs can take large amounts of disk space, so you should also have a log rotation and retention policy.

Logging Tools

Many logging tools exist. Some allow for log aggregation, where logs from multiple systems can be combined into a single log. As logs become larger and more complex, log parsing becomes increasingly important. You need to be able to parse out information pertinent to what you are looking for. One common logging technology is RADIUS. RADIUS provides technology-independent logging for hardware devices and applications. Windows includes Windows Event Viewer to provide logging functionality.

Windows Event Viewer

The Event Viewer has long been the central repository for logging in Windows systems. Windows 7 and Windows Server 2008 R2 are no exceptions. Event Viewer allows you to get a better look at what's really going on with your system. You can see user information, application information, and system information. The amount of information that can be collected in Event Viewer can be somewhat overwhelming. This is why it's important to have a good understanding of what is logged where and why. Having this understanding will allow you to better focus your efforts. Event Viewer can be accessed by going to Start>All Programs>Administrative Tools>Event Viewer. You can also access Event Viewer by adding the Event Viewer snap-in to a custom MMC console.

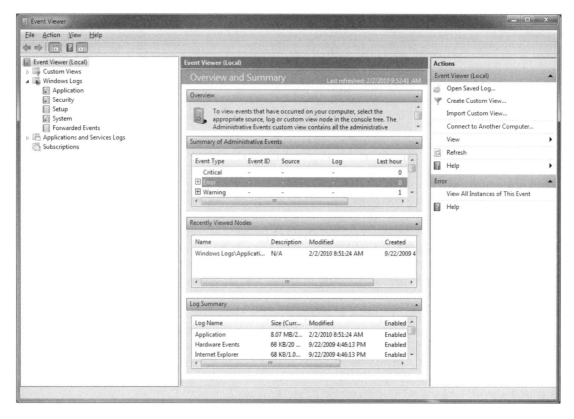

Figure 6.18 Event Viewer Overview and Summary.

Overview and Summary: When you open Event Viewer, you are presented with the Overview and Summary view, as shown in Figure 6.18. The Overview and Summary view gives you a summary of the events that have happened within Event Viewer.

At the top you have the Summary of Administrative Events. This is a summary of all the events that have been logged to Event Viewer. The events are ordered by event type, then subordered by even ID, and then by source. This can help you to determine what types of issues most often plague your system. The Summary of Administrative Events section also allows you to view all occurrences of a certain event. Simply right-click the event and select **View All Instances of This Event**. You will then be presented with a summary page that has all occurrences of this event listed.

You also have the Recently Viewed Nodes section. This section will list any default logs or custom views you have displayed while in Event Viewer. If you want to return to a particular view, simply right-click the view and select **View events in this custom view/log**. You will then be taken to that view.

Finally, you have the Log Summary section. This section gives you the properties of all the logs being tracked in Event Viewer. You can see the name of the log, the size, when it was last modified, if the log is enabled or disabled, and the retention policy for the log.

Windows Logs: The Windows Log section is what most people are used to seeing in a typical Event Viewer session. These logs represent logging for the basic functionalities within Windows. Items logged to the Windows Logs will have the following information associated with them:

- **Level** This option represents the logging level of the event. It contains information, warning, error, or critical levels. Critical being the most serious.
- **Keywords** This is seen in the Security Log. It denotes the type of event logged. It will either be audit success or audit failure.
- **Date and Time** This is the date and time the event was logged.
- **Source** This will tell you which module or subsystem reported the information.
- **Event ID** Each different type of Event Viewer log entry has a different Event ID. This option will help you to better understand the nature of the log entry.
- **Task Category** If there is a task associated with an event log entry, it should be associated with a category. This will help you to understand the nature of the entry and a possible cause.

When you open an entry in Event Viewer, you will be taken to the General tab of the Event Properties window, as shown in Figure 6.19. You will be able to see all the general information

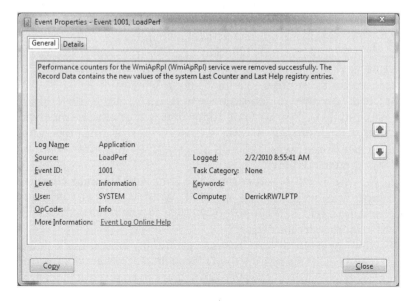

Figure 6.19 Event Properties – General tab.

associated with the event. You will see Log Name, Source, Event ID, Level, User, OpCode, Logged (date and time), Task Category, Keywords, and Computer. You also have the choice of using Online Help to view more information about the entry. Event Viewer will also give you the option to copy the contents of the event so that it can be pasted somewhere else, like within an e-mail.

There are five logs in the Windows Logs section: Application, Security, Setup, System and, Forwarded Events.

- **Application Log** The Application Log is where you can find information about applications that are running on your system. You can find information about Windows 7 applications, other Microsoft applications, and various third-party applications. The Application log is very useful in determining why an application is not functioning properly.
- **Setup Log** The Setup Log is for certain setup and installation events. For example, certain Windows Update initiated installations will be logged.
- **System Log** The System Log will show events logged by the operating system and Windows services. The System Log can be used to determine what services didn't start and possibly why they didn't start.
- **Forwarded Events** The Forwarded Events Log allows you to aggregate logs from many different systems into one place. The Forwarded Events Log will show event entries sent to the computer from other computers. This log is disabled by default. In order to receive entries in the Forwarded Events log, you must enable subscriptions and subscribe to a remote system.

Configuring Forwarded Events in Windows Event Viewer

1. Right-click the **Forwarded Events log** and select **Properties**.
2. Click the **Subscriptions tab**, as shown in Figure 6.20.
3. On the Subscriptions tab, select **Create**. This will bring up the Subscription Properties window, as shown in Figure 6.21.
4. Give your subscription a name and a description.
5. Next, you have to determine where you want the subscription to initiate from and which computers you want to be involved. For this example, we will choose **Collector initiated**. Click **Select Computers**. This will bring up the Computers window, as shown in Figure 6.22.
6. Now we need to add computers. Click **Add Domain computers**. This brings up the standard Windows Select Computer window. Add the computers you want to be a part of the subscription and click **OK**.
7. Now we need to specify what events to collect. Click **Select Events**. This brings up the Query Filter window, as shown in Figure 6.23. Select the events you want to collect and click **OK**.

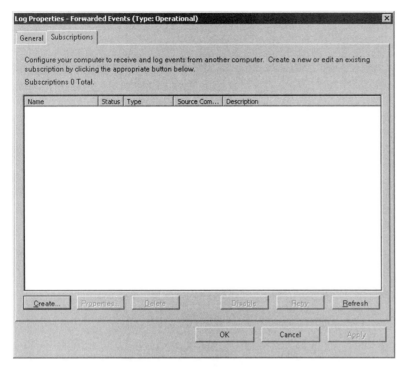

Figure 6.20 Event Viewer Subscriptions tab.

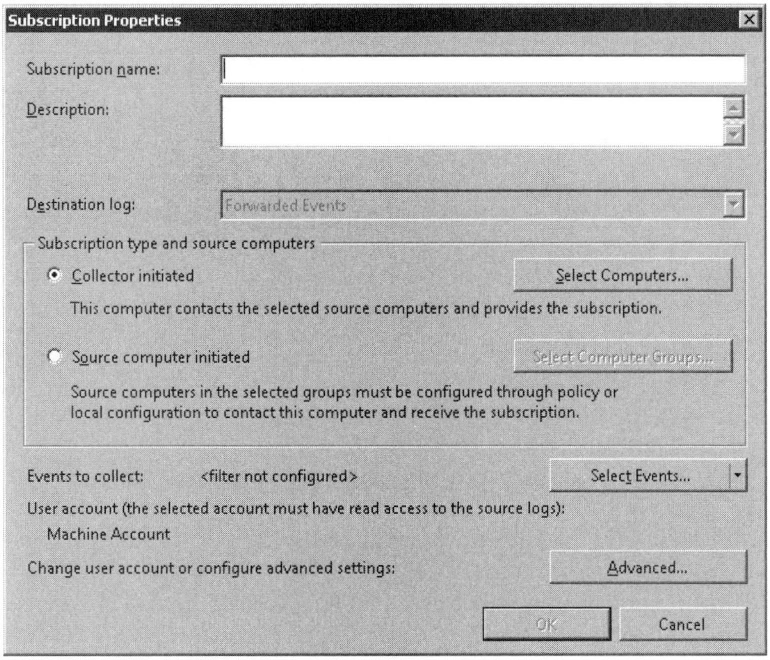

Figure 6.21 Event Viewer Subscription Properties window.

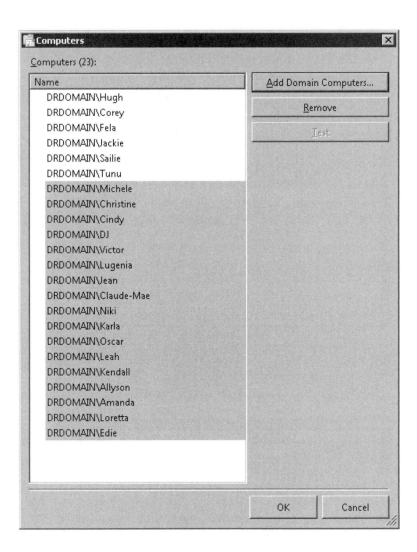

Figure 6.22 Event Viewer Computers window.

8. Clicking the **Advanced** button will bring up the Advanced Subscription Settings window, as shown in Figure 6.24. For here, you can configure advanced options like which user account to use to read the logs.

9. Click **OK**. Your subscription will now show up in the Subscriptions window.

10. Click **OK**. You will now begin receiving events on your Forwarded Events Log.

Applications and Services Logs: The Applications and Services Logs are a collection of logs that offer information about specific

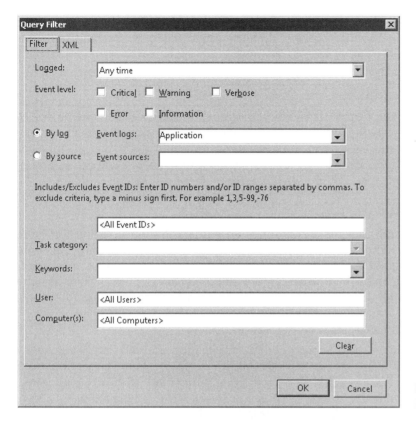

Figure 6.23 Event Viewer Query Filter window.

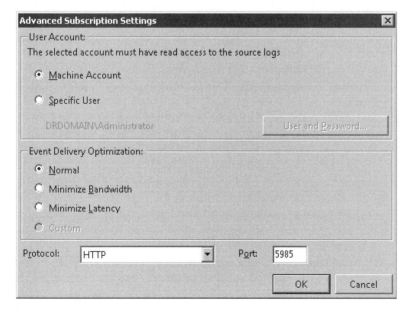

Figure 6.24 Event Viewer Advanced Subscription Settings window.

services and specific applications. Each of these applications and services has its own log. Simply view the log for the application or service you want more information on.

Auditing

Auditing is very similar to logging. In fact, auditing often involves reviewing log files. The main difference is that auditing is usually user or security related. Auditing usually involves tracking user access and rights usage. When auditing user access rights, generally you can choose to audit successes, failures, or both.

Auditing Tools

Auditing tools come in many different shapes and sizes. Some auditing tools provide for centralized auditing, some don't. Some audit tools can send alerts when preselected events take place. Windows provides two main tools for auditing. They are the Windows Event Viewer and the Local Security Policy applications.

Local Security Policy application

The Local Security Policy application contains an Audit Policy section and an Advance Audit Policy Configuration section. Both sections allow for security auditing, but the Advanced Audit Policy Configuration section, as shown in Figure 6.25, allows for more granular audit controls. This is the section we will cover. The Advanced Audit Policy Configuration section has 10 sections:

- **Account Logon** This section allows you to audit credential validation, account logon events, Kerberos authentication events, and Kerberos ticketing events.
- **Account Management** This section allows you to audit changes to user accounts, groups, and computer accounts.
- **Detailed Tracking** This section allows you to audit DPAPI, process creation, process termination, and RPC events.
- **DS Access** This section allows you to audit Directory Service access, changes, and replication.
- **Logon/Logoff** This section allows you to audit account lockouts, IPSec events, logons, and logoffs.
- **Object Access** This section allows you to audit file shares, certification services, the registry, kernel object access, and many other objects.
- **Policy Change** This section allows you to audit changes in the authentication policy, authorization policy, and other policy change events.

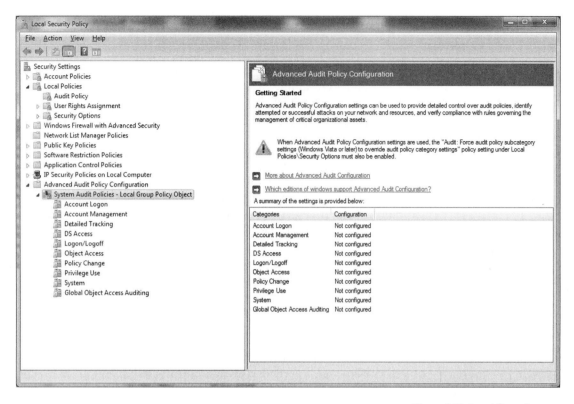

Figure 6.25 Local Security Policy Application – Advanced Audit Policy.

- **Privilege Use** This section allows you to audit the use of user privileges.
- **System** This section allows you to audit the IPSec driver, security state changes, system integrity, and other system events.
- **Global Object Access Auditing** This section allows you to audit registry and file system changes.

Windows Event Viewer – Security Logs

The Windows Event Viewer contains a Security Logs section that can be used for security auditing. The Security Log holds auditing events. You can audit everything from system access to file access. You will see success events and failure events. The Security Log is very useful in trying to determine if someone is trying to gain access to your system. The Security Log can also help you to determine if an application is trying to access something it doesn't have rights to or if it is trying to perform a function it does not have a right to do. This can be a sign of malicious activity.

Summary

Security audits and assessments help to give you the confidence that your environment is secure and free from compromise. Periodic vulnerability assessments can be used to help to determine how susceptible your environment is to attack and failures. The information gained from a vulnerability assessment can be used to help to prevent attacks and compromises.

A good monitoring policy will help you to understand the current state of your systems. This will help you to determine if your systems are currently under attack. It will also help you to determine possible vulnerabilities on your systems. If your systems are low on resources, then it wouldn't be too difficult for someone to perform a denial-of-service attack. Monitoring will help to pinpoint whether systems need memory, more processing power, and so on.

You can't always be there to examine your systems in real time. This is where logging and auditing come into place. Logging and auditing help you to determine what events have been occurring on your system when you weren't actively monitoring it. They also help you to identify patterns of normal and abnormal system behavior. Many times even if a specific compromise isn't detected, the discovery of abnormal behavior can help alert you of an incident.

APPENDIX A: COMMON APPLICATIONS AND PORT NUMBERS

Protocol/Application	Port Number
DHCP	UDP 67 (sending), 68 (receiving)
DNS	UDP, TCP 53
FTP	TCP 21
HTTP	TCP 80
HTTPS	TCP 443
ICA (CGP)	TCP 1494 (2598)
LDAP	TCP 389
LDAPS	TCP 636
LDAP(S) to Active Directory Global Catalog	TCP 3268, 3269
POP3	110
RADIUS Authentication	UDP 1812, 1645
RADIUS Accounting	UDP 1813, 1646
RDP and Terminal Services	TCP 3389
RPC Locator Service	TCP 135
SSH	TCP 22
SMTP	TCP 25
SNMP	UDP 161
SQL Server	TCP 1433
TACACS+	UDP/TCP 49
Telnet	TCP 23
WINS	TCP 137
WINS Replication	TCP 42

Security for Microsoft Windows System Administrators. DOI: 10.1016/B978-1-59749-594-3.00007-7

APPENDIX B: INFORMATION SECURITY PROFESSIONAL CERTIFICATIONS

Certification can help show your proficiency in the area of certification. There are security certifications that are technology and vendor neutral, and there are those that focus on specific vendors or technologies. Security certifications can be advantageous for people who do not have security titles. Certifications will help show potential employers proficiency in security areas.

Microsoft

Microsoft certifications cover a wide range of areas. There are certifications for developers, administrators, and architects. Microsoft has two security-related systems certifications: MCSA (Microsoft Certified Systems Administrator) Security and MCSE (Microsoft Certified Systems Engineer) Security. If you want more information on Microsoft or Microsoft certifications, you can visit the Microsoft Web site at www.microsoft.com/learning.

CompTIA

CompTIA is the Computing Technology Industry Association. CompTIA has long been known for its array of vendor-neutral certifications.

CompTIA offers a vendor-neutral security certification called *Security+*. The CompTIA Security+ certification requires that the candidates pass a single exam. This exam will test the candidate's knowledge in the areas of system security, network security, access control, and organizational security. CompTIA recommends that the candidates have at least two years of experience with an emphasis on security before taking the exam. If you would like more information about CompTIA or its certifications, you can visit its Web site at www.comptia.org.

Security for Microsoft Windows System Administrators. DOI: 10.1016/B978-1-59749-594-3.00008-9

(ISC)²

(ISC)² is the International Information Systems Security Certification Consortium. The (ISC)² is headquartered in the United States and has offices in London, Hong Kong, and Tokyo. The (ISC)² offers vendor-neutral security certifications. These certifications range from intermediate to advanced.

The (ISC)² currently offers the following certifications: SSCP (Systems Security Certified Practitioner), CAP (Certification and Accreditation Professional), CSSLP (Certified Secure Software Lifecycle Professional), CISSP (Certified Information Systems Security Professional), and various CISSP concentrations. Currently, CISSP concentrations include ISSAP (Information Systems Security Architecture Professional), ISSEP (Information Systems Security Engineering Professional), and ISSMP (Information Systems Security Management Professional). (ISC)² certifications generally require passing an exam, a work experience requirement, and an endorsement from someone with a current (ISC)² certification. If you want more information about the (ISC)² or (ISC)² certifications, you can visit the (ISC)² Web site at www.(isc2).org.

GIAC

The GIAC is the Global Information Assurance Certification. The GIAC was established to certify the skills of security professionals. The GIAC offers advanced-level security certifications. The GIAC has multiple certifications in a wide range of security areas. If you want to find out more about the GIAC or GIAC certifications, you can visit the GIAC Web site at www.giac.org.

ISACA

The ISACA is the Information Systems Audit and Control Association. The ISACA is an international organization that was established in 1967. The ISACA offers a wide range of Information Systems certifications.

The ISACA offers the following certifications: CISM (Certified Information Security Manager), CISA (Certified Information Security Auditor), CGEIT (Certified in the Governance of Enterprise IT), and CRISC (Certified in Risk and Information Systems Control). If you want to find out more information about the ISACA or ISACA certifications, you can visit the ISACA Web site at www.isaca.org.

INDEX

Page numbers followed by *f* indicates a figure and *t* indicates a table.